One and eightpence
in my Pocket

June Pickerill

June Pickerill

One and eightpence in My Pocket

by
June Pickerill

First published in Great Britain 2002
by The LICHFIELD PRESS

ISBN 090598531 1

The LICHFIELD PRESS
City House, 2 Dam Street
LICHFIELD
Staffs., W513 6AA
United Kingdom

This book is dedicated to my grandchildren

Joe, Helena, Sam and Chloë
to give them a notion of their own history

INTRODUCTION

I have been involved with research into the life of John Pickering since 1980 and always in the back of my mind there has been the nagging compulsion to "put it all down on paper", the ultimate goal.

Every time I have toyed with the idea, excuses have floated through my brain - I haven't got the time, I really must find out about this or that I don't have enough details of the situation - I have not accumulated the necessary background information- all designed to put off the day of reckoning.

There are gaps, more than I even realised, there probably always will be, and I do not profess to be an expert on background material. I have tried to keep rigidly to the facts as they are known to me, and not to fill the background with my imagination. I may have raised a few questions, which I hope might be filled with a few answers, apart from that I make no excuses, only that time marches on and pen at some time, either sooner, or later, has to be committed to paper. I have searched my mind for a very long time on the way to tackle this project, and have come to the conclusion that the obvious approach is the only way: start at the beginning, carry on until the end, and then stop. So here goes.

Chapter 1

This true story is about a man, who is not to my knowledge, recorded
in any history books, who was tragically killed, and whose body was
never recovered from the depths of the ocean. However, his impact on
Australia's history is significant by the number of descendants he
generated, and the pioneering spirit which was evident during the
short space of fourteen years he spent in South Australia.

His story survived by a series of events which by themselves are not
significant, but combined present a delicate spider's web, encompass-
ing all the necessary requirements for his story to float to the surface
one hundred and fifty years later.

Given none of these events, his life, and that of his family, would
have sunk to oblivion along with his body.

Was it mere chance that he was literate at a time when most of his
contemporaries were illiterate? He wrote home at regular intervals,
giving a superb picture of life as a pioneer. He neither boasted or
exaggerated, making research from a distance of thousands of miles
more easy than it could have been. Everything he wrote was hard
solid fact.

These letters were safely delivered, at a time when ships were
frequently lost at sea, and were safely stored away, albeit for a
hundred and fifty years.

The last people in the family line who were responsible for clearing
away an accumulation of sixty years of living in one place, were my
husband and myself. Had my husband drawn the short straw of clearing a huge housekeeper's cupboard, papers (and these letters) would
have been cleared in one movement. Fortunately the job fell to me,
and with a lot of patience, opening every bit of paper

7

and inspecting each piece, these letters forced their way into the daylight.

I was not at that time interested in genealogy, with no knowledge of even the basic elements of research, but have been blessed (or cursed depending on which way you look at it), with a very curious mind, and a lot of dogged persistence. The seeds had indeed been sown in the right place.

This man was determined to have his rightful place in Australia's history, and has given me no resting place since that fateful day. Any peace of mind that is due to me, will not be resolved until "the records have been set straight".

On a sad day in April 1980, my family and I were required to look for relevant documents to enable us to register the death of Ruth Helena Pickerill, my husband's aunt, and last remaining relative. Unfortunately by the age of nineteen, my husband had lost both Mother and Father, and had then lived until the time of our marriage with Aunt Nell. As he was the only close relative, we had the onerous task of dealing with everything there is to do when one is confronted by a death in the family. We decided that the easiest way of finding the necessary certificates was to empty all the drawers and cupboards into a clothes basket and take them home to sort at our leisure. Little did I know that my hobbies and interests would be completely changed overnight.

A rusty cocoa tin had been found right at the back of an old housekeeper's cupboard, untouched for years. In it were some papers tied with a dirty length of tape. Being very methodical, we decided to flatten every piece of folded paper, and open and empty every envelope. It took hours of patience, but what treasures were revealed. The tape was undone, and old tissuelike paper was very carefully opened to reveal an amazing story. My daughter and I sat and tried to read a collection of nine letters, written phonetically, about a pioneering life in South Australia from 1849 to 1864, by a

8

man who called himself John Pickering, written to his father, John Pickering, Old Road, Cannock.

We were becoming confused. Our surname was Pickerill, and Pickering was another name altogether. I might add at that time we had not entered the world of genealogy and were not familiar with the vagaries of surname spelling in the nineteenth century and earlier.

Fortunately, a couple of years earlier, I had sat down with Aunt Nell and drawn a family tree backwards just as far as her father. He had been married twice and she was the youngest child of the second marriage. This had been done purely to save me from confusion when relatives were mentioned that were unknown to me - my husband was no help, he was as confused as me. I would keep this piece of white card handy, and when necessary would consult it to make sense of relationships.

That was our starting point.

We made the fortunate decision to work backwards a generation at a time, and this is where our luck came in: the family had been static in Cannock, Staffordshire, from 1752 and we found it comparatively easy to draw a comprehensive family tree, without any formal tuition. Call it beginner's luck, but we were hooked.

It soon became obvious that John Pickering, Australia, was also John Pickerill, late of Cannock. Like a good jigsaw, pieces began fitting together without being forced, and family details from the first letters corresponded with amazing clarity to the research we had started to conduct. We were not without problems, however. It took us more than six years to find his birth, but every bit of information uncovered only confirmed that Pickering and Pickerill were one and the same family. John Pickrell (note the spelling) was baptised on 20 May, 1820 at Holy Trinity Church, Baswich, Stafford, fourth child and second son of John and Hannah Pickarel (two different spellings on one certificate), the mother's maiden name being Withnall. Joseph, Aunt Nell's father, was John's brother, youngest child of the family, baptised 14 February, 1830 at St. Luke's Parish Church, Cannock. John and Hannah raised the first six children at Brocton, a village near Stafford, where Hannah's parents lived. As the area was, and still is, rural, it is possible that farming of some sort was carried on by the family. On 15 September 1825, Christopher Pickeril (another spelling), the father of John, cordwainer, died at Cannock, the Pickerill family home, leaving property and land there in his will, to his son. An original legal document, leaving land to Elizabeth his daughter, dated 1827 states "Christopher Pickering (later referred to as Christopher Pickrell) of Cannock, Cordwainer" throws the surname into utter confusion. So far, the earliest surname in 1752 is recorded as Christopher Pickerhill. As the seventh child, Jane, was born on 19 March 1825, at Cannock, and two subsequent children, made a total of nine in family, it is reasonable to assume that the conditions of the will brought about the change of residence. When John was almost eleven years of age, his mother died, leaving a family of nine, the youngest, Joseph, only twelve months old.

Sometime during the next few years John would have been apprenticed to a brickmaker, who could possibly have been his Uncle George Tomlinson, married to his father's sister Jane, living in property nearby.

George was a much respected member of the community, being appointed Surveyor of the Highways for 1845/46, and holding the position of Overseer for the Poor. He was a brickmaker and bricklayer and was given the contract in 1835 to build a lock-up house in Cannock, and in 1841 to build a wall around the churchyard of St. Luke's Parish Church, Cannock: also to repair the parapet on the south side of the church.*

On 8 August 1847, John's father, a widower for over sixteen years, married at St. Luke's Parish Church, Cannock, Mary Brue from Bradley in the Black Country.

A month later, on 26 September 1847, John married Sarah Ann Sanders, at the parish church in Bloxwich. According to the Marriage Certificate, he was a brickmaker by trade, and at the time of his marriage, was living at Bentley Hey, near Walsall, Staffordshire. Sarah was aged 25 years, "living at home", with her father Joseph.

Sarah was born in 1822 near Wednesbury, Staffordshire, of parents "whose leanings were towards religion and religious privileges. Consequently, she became acquainted with Christian teaching and duty in early life. In her youth she attended the services of Gold's Green Primitive Methodist Chapel, Darlaston Circuit, which was at that time in a very prosperous state. She soon joined that steady and working Society, and became a prominent and useful member in the class and prayer meetings. About this time she became acquainted with John who was a local preacher". **

That he was a local preacher has yet to be proved, but from the tone of his letters home, and the references made, he was also a Primitive Methodist,*** with a great interest in "the Bretheren at Hednesford" and friends at Podgy Lane, Cannock, both early Primitive Methodist centres. John Pickering would have been regarded as something of a rebel, but perhaps not by his family. His grandfather, Christopher and father John, could well have shared

*Cannock Vestry Order Book 1812-47   **South Australian Primitive Methodist Record July 1885
***Methodists, so called from the methodical way they organised themselves. were followers of John Wesley. When the Church of England turned against him, Wesley travelled the country on horseback for fifty years, taking the church to the people. Hugh Bourne. a native of Stoke-on-Trent and a Methodist felt compelled to return to the basics of Christianity and thus the primitive Methodists were born. The Government was naturally suspicious of the two-day meetings he held attended by thousands, at a time when the country was at war with revolutionary France

his views, as both were, by trade, cordwainers (shoemakers) and cordwainers were known for their leanings towards dissent. Maybe during their working hours, mostly in their own company, they would have plenty of thinking time without rules and regulations to influence them.

It is interesting to note that Joseph, John's youngest brother, and his family, worshipped at St. Luke's Parish Church, and in later years rented their own family pew, giving the impression that he, at any rate, did not share his brother's views on forms of worship, and was eager to conform to the establishment.

John's father, also John,
the recipient of the letters

John now becomes something of an enigma, as the reasons for his emigration to South Australia in 1849 are not obvious. It is therefore fairly safe to assume that his religious leanings did not meet with approval from a large percentage of the local community, and he might have felt frustrated at being on the fringe of society, as religious intolerance was high at this point in England's history. However, on the other side of the world, South Australia was becoming known as "The Paradise of Dissent" meaning that one was free to worship as one chose.

Of course, as he would have been able to read the newspapers of the day, John would also have realised that it was possible through hard work, to make the kind of money in South Australia only dreamed of by the working classes in England. Posters were issued as early as February 1839 and advertisements appeared in newspapers, urging anyone with a trade to apply for a free passage, with twenty-one desired occupations listed. The agents were interested specifically in receiving applications from married couples (or alternatively single men to be accompanied by their single sisters) under the age of thirty. However, agents would sometimes encourage couples well over the age limit to apply for a free passage.

Her Majesty's Colonial Land and Emigration Commissioners also issued "Colonization Circulars" between 1843 to 1873, covering the Colonies of North America, Falkland Islands, West Indies, Australia, Van Dieman's Land, Cape of Good Hope, New Zealand, Natal, Ceylon and Hong Kong. These contained advice on climate, population, demand for labour, wages, cost of passage, where to find Emigration Agents etc.

The Enclosures Act introduced by Parliament between 1760 and 1820 reduced the yeoman class of small landowning farmers to agricultural labourers, or forced them to leave the land, and which applied to a quarter of England. This had made the farming community resentful, and obstacles rather than opportunities seemed to be the order of the day. A bad outbreak of cholera in Walsall and surrounding areas had also occurred in 1839 claiming very many lives and wiping out entire families. The "Colonization Circulars" stated that in South Australia "There is no endemic disease: intermittent fevers are scarce, tubercular affections of the lungs are infrequent and epidemic cholera has not visited the colony". All these events may have culminated in a longing to escape and make a better life for himself and his family.

However, the overriding desire to "be his own master" is evident from the tone in his letters home, but always the intention was to make his fortune in South Australia and come back home and buy, not rent, a farm of his own.

How many times had John and Sarah, and their families, discussed this possibility and turned the idea over in their minds the undertaking of this huge adventure? Was it a joint decision? Or did John take the final responsibility for his actions? Did they pray together asking for guidance and help in making the most important decision of their lives? And pray together with a wider congregation, before John made the momentous decision to sail on his own to an unknown country, on the other side of the world, leaving behind him his new wife, his family, his friends, his job, and finally his church?

Chapter 2

The passenger list in South Australia states that John Pickering sailed "last from Plymouth" on the 925 tons "Stebonheath" under the command of John Sargeant on 31 January 1849. Passengers in the cabin were Mr. C. Cooper and wife, Mr. H. Trison Jones and wife, Messrs. Thrapp, Hastie, Walker, Chapman, and James, Mr. Hirvins, Surgeon-Superintendent, and Mrs. Lowe, Head Matron, and 373 emigrants mainly from London. This suggests that the ship started its journey from London.

A journey from the Midlands to London would have been more straightforward than Plymouth. He would have been able to travel either by stage coach, by canal network from Penkridge, or alternatively by the developing railways.

Rail travel initially was very expensive and a journey to London would have cost more than his passage to Australia, but a new allowance had been made for passengers of limited means to travel at the rate of one penny a mile, therefore the cost of the journey to London would have amounted to little more that ten shillings or half a gold sovereign. As the railways had been laid at Penkridge in 1834 and was within walking distance of Cannock, his journey could well have started at the station there, changing at Wolverhampton for London.

As the last port of call made by the "Stebonheath" was Plymouth, it is likely that Cornish miners would join the ship there to start their big adventure in the copper mines of Burra Burra in South Australia, joining friends who had already taken the challenge.

15

It is not known whether John paid his own passage, although family legend says that he did, or he might well have been assisted by the Government, and a guess can only be made about the conditions experienced on board ship. However, one thing is certain, he was given plenty of time during the weeks of tossing about on the vast ocean, to think things over and have doubts about the wisdom of his decision.

Often people travelled together in groups of friends, so maybe there was someone else from Cannock who travelled with him, which would have made easier the long, long journey. He may have suffered from terrible sickness, and been witness to fellow passengers losing their lives from disease, as cholera, scarlatina, whooping cough, diarrhoea and dysentery were very often rife on board ship, and there would be a strong possibility of someone losing their life by drowning. He would certainly have seen new life being brought into the world.

Did his faith and religious conviction give him the strength to overcome all these hardships suffered by these early emigrants, and enable him to help others less fortunate than himself?

As we do not have any kind of record of the journeys made by John in 1849, or Sarah and her son in 1854, only a guess can be made at the kind of traumas, pleasures and adventures they experienced while on board ship. However, from a very detailed log written by a steerage passenger, single, twenty-seven year old Nation Braine, who sailed from Liverpool in November 1865 to Sydney, Australia, we can, through his eyes, form a picture of what appears to be a fairly typical voyage, and in his own words...

On arrival at the port of departure, passengers would have been required to present their shipping papers at the Emigration Depot, together with another three or four hundred men, women and children of different nationalities "some singing and dancing, others looking sad." Accommodation was under the same roof, the bell ringing at 9. 0 p.m. to signal bedtime. The married families and single girls were segregated from the single men, the beds being arranged like berths in a ship. Next morning, after making their own beds, and getting dressed (if they had undressed the previous night) they assembled in the mess room downstairs "where we all look at each other like strange cats in a garret." After visiting the wash houses for a wash and brush, the bell would ring for breakfast. Everyone formed into messes of ten and were given a number of tickets which enabled them to have about 7oz. butter and 9 or 10lb. of good bread and as much tea as they could drink. "We ask a blessing of the Lord then eat like wolves and leave the empties like pigs. After that some write letters, others play dominoes or sing and dance. Married women wash their children while their husbands smoke and sing, or anything to kill the time".

Their boxes which had been left at the station were delivered to them at a charge of 4d. per box.

The bell rings for dinner at 1.30p.m. and consists of about "6lb of good fresh hot beef and beautiful soup". No one was allowed to leave the Depot in case they stayed away too long. "Their (sic) is plenty of life here and music and many smiling and gloomy faces. Children crying, women laughing, men smoking not caring for anyone."

Teatime consists of the same food as breakfast, although the tea is very weak and is the last meal till bedtime. Letters are delivered twice a day at 1.0 p.m. and 5. 0 p.m.

On the second day at the Depot, the Doctor carried out the examinations for small pox and entered their names, young women first, then married couples and then single men.

The ship is lying alongside the Depot loading, and ten of the young male passengers are picked out to arrange the beds and hammocks in all parts of the ship, and work until 4p.m. "She is a monster inside. It would surprise some land men to see her. She is a sight and she is beautifully arranged for comforts in all ways". After tea and letters are delivered, "we go to bed like soldiers to a barrack room, full of noisy jokes, dancing and singing, for some were never so well off in their lives or fed so well."

On the third day they are served with two canvas bags, three feet long and eighteen inches wide. The bags have a number stamped on them which is the same as the one on the hammock on the ship. Also served are the mess utensils which consist of a pint cup made of tin, one plate, knife and fork, teaspoon, tablespoon, and every captain of each mess receives the cooking ware. The boxes are searched for spirits or articles not allowed in the Articles of Embarkation and are then put aboard ship and stored in the hold. Passengers are then allowed access about every four weeks throughout the journey.

At 4p.m. orders were given for all to go on board to have tea and sleep that night, and that would be the last time land would be touched until they all reached Australia.

"It was a sight to see. Nearly 500 men, women and children going up the plank with their bags on their shoulders. Aboard this monster of a ship some people would wonder where they all got to and when they were aboard you could not see a third of them."

Everyone formed into a mess of ten with a Captain to each mess and he was expected to get out of bed before 7a.m. to collect the allowance of water and bread before breakfast at 8a.m.

And so they set sail. "The order is now given by the Pilot to cast off her bow rope. All was on deck to see our mighty ship move from her moorings. There was three cheers given for Old England and Ireland and the Captain, and she slowly moved to the dock gates."

Everything on board seemed very well organised and the passengers seemed to respond very well. Breakfast at 8a.m. Dinner 12.30-1p.m. Tea 5p.m. Prayers at 8p.m. and Bedtime at 10p.m. The menu repeated itself every week:

Sunday - Boiled salt pork, soup and duff
Monday - Salt beef and vegetables.
Tuesday - Preserved beef and rice.
Wednesday - Pork, soup and plum duff also plain suet duff
Thursday - Salt beef
Friday - Preserved meat.
Saturday - Pork
Three sorts of meat, beef, both salt and preserved, pork and mutton, with plenty of salt, pepper and mustard, and two and a half pints of good mixed pickles between the mess of ten, once a week, with the baker on board baking fresh bread on Tuesdays, Fridays and Sundays. Each passenger was allowed three quarts of water a day from which was deducted three pints for tea, breakfast water and soup, the remainder for personal use. No beer allowed. 6oz. of biscuits and 8oz. flour plus half a pound of fresh bread and half a pound of meat three times a week were distributed to each passenger.

To make the plum duff each mess had 5lb. of raisins each week - 1lb10oz two days a week - 1lb 4oz. one day and none on Tuesdays - just plain duff, with each mess cooking their own, having their own day for baking.

Thursday was the day for serving out the weekly allowances to each mess and which had to be carefully packed away.
10oz. Tea
20oz. Coffee
1/4 lb. moist sugar

4lbs. Molasses lqt. Lime juice
21/2 pts mixed pickles
3oz. mustard
3oz. pepper 1lb. salt
31b 12 oz. salt butter

The passengers were strictly segregated with the single women in the 'after part' of the ship, married couples and their children 'midships' and all the single men in the 'fore part'. On this particular ship it is noticeable that there was a larger proportion of single girls i.e. 1 - 23 mess single girls' department, 24 - 32 mess married department and 33-47 mess single men's department. Even for worship, which took place every Sunday morning at 11a.m. the Protestants went into the married department, the Catholics remained in the single men's department and the single girls remained where they were.

"Two strong men were picked out who act as constables for to see to our comforts... .We have also four constables for single women (but not to be with them) only to attend to galley and fetch their rations for them for they must not go abaft the main mast nor us young men are not to be abaft the Galley and the married people divide us so there won't be no courting, only by dum(sic) motion signals".

Some hammocks were used for sleeping purposes, particularly in the single men's department, and these caused great hilarity at times, and also injury. "Our hammocks are ready slung over our heads to show them the way how to sling them... then comes the scene to see some of the coves falling out of their hammocks and the comic way of some getting into them. At last all got in safe and went to sleep until about three in the morning when an old Irish man near us fell out and was took to the hospital." During darkness three lamps were lit in the single men's quarters and burned all night. The hammocks were called out by number before bedtime and put all together in the bunk head in the morning. Every week or so, depending on the suitability of the weather, orders were issued at 9a.m. for each passenger to take his or her bed on deck for an airing. "It was a funny sight to see nearly 450 passengers with their beds. It reminds me of the portion of scripture that says 'take up thy bed and walk' only on a larger scale."

Twelve passengers were taken from each department every day, in rotation to sweep the floors, their turn occurring about once every ten days. "It's my mess sweeping day. We have to sweep and clean our department in turns. We clean and sweep up after every meal. It's our first time to sweep. There are many jokes passed during this operation. Its more fun than work." Passengers were also required to take a turn at scrubbing the deck which was seen as not a very pleasant but necessary job.

A storm which supplied the ship with rainwater was considered a blessing, as it was then used for washing of clothes on deck. A month after setting sail, "up early, washed and break-fast being over I have to go to the wash tub for necessity compels me for I have a bag full of clothing. A friend of mine gives me some soap suds which is of value here. It's a scarce thing water on board ship, except salt water and that we get too much of at times on deck. I now wash my shirts and jackets out and they look fine and clean. They are now blowing in a fine breeze from the rigging. They will soon be dry".

The ship possessed a steam engine and an engineer for condensing the sea water into fresh and could condense 800 gallons of water a day. There was a tank on board with a capacity of 137,000 gallons which was filled with fresh water on leaving England. Her other cargo consisted of beer and porter, slates and other general cargo, amounting in total to 2000 tons.

After being on board for a month, passengers realised that a great many articles were being missed from their bags and so a watch was set up every night, four men a night taking it in turns, divided into two watches. "It's the safest plan."

The passengers' luggage, other than that stored in their two canvas bags, was stored in their boxes in the hold of the ship~ These were brought up about every four weeks for items to be taken out and others packed away. Again this was achieved in a very organised fashion, with single girls obtaining their boxes in the morning and married couples at 2p.m. Single men had to wait until the following morning. Passengers could only have them in their possession for half an hour and they were then collected and put back in the hold. All this was very necessary, for on the long journey to Australia, they went through several extreme changes of climate - from very cold to very hot, and needed to change heavy clothing for lighter garments, and vice versa. The condition of the contents left much to be desired. "The ladies' dresses and silks all mildewed and they blowing up their husbands as though they could help it and the same with the men's clothing. They were very bad all of them." There were all sorts of luxuries such as hams, lumps of butter, bags of flour in 30 and 40lb, saveloys, cheese, jams, plum puddings, cakes, pickles, bacon and lots of tobacco. One man from Ireland brought nearly a bushel of potatoes. One young man had a quart bottle of whisky put by and somehow or other he lost it and "after an hour or so two or three Irish chaps were seen nearly tight that looks very suspicious. It caused a great bother".

As the weather changed, so did the clothing and what passengers did not possess they made. "I assist one of my mates after breakfast to make a pair of white trousers out of one of his sheets for it's very warm now for heavy trousers. I save cutting my sheets up for I buy a pair for 1/7d. of my next door neighbours and very good ones. I get the cutting of the sheet and makes three good white caps.

"We have many ready made tailors at work making white trousers from their sheets. I expect to see some guys dressed on Sunday morning church time for we have to pass the Doctor to see if we are clean and respectable... I have my white trousers and jacket and cap. Some are like me in light suits others in black suits and some in their flannel vests. I only regretted I was not an artist to of sketched the motley group on deck as they mustered. Some were in light suits large enough for two such men while others' suits were too small for them. One of our mates had lately purchased a panama straw hat off one of the sailors for 8/6d. and he wore it this morning which made the scene more pantomimeic."

When all the necessary chores had been completed it was left to the individual to decide how best to spend the rest of the time. Music was very much to the fore, with different kinds of wind and string instruments, and was used to accompany dancing polkas, waltzes and Irish jigs. There was also a lot of singing, with the sailors joining in. "We have a jolly lot of sailors on board. They sing a good song." Board games were also played. "After dinner some goes to cards and others to dominoes and draughts and chess and various other dozen games. I hear one man near me losses about two soverins at cards."

A lot of time was passed sitting smoking, and those that could read made use of the Library. "17th Dec. We opened our Library yesterday. I was too late to draw a book. You are to keep them a week and return them every Saturday."

For passengers willing to learn, "20th Dec. Our school commences yesterday in all parts of the ship. There are plenty of books, slates, and pencils. I don't require it myself but it's a good thing for some. Some that cannot read or write or cipher. It's fun to see some educated little boys teaching men old enough to be their fathers. Many bits of fun happens during school hours."

From time to time a concert was held, weather permitting, and, to try and cure the boredom, raffles were organised. "One of my mess maits (sic) is wichful(sic) to raise the private capital to land in Sydney, so he is going to raise enough members at 6d. each to amount to £2 for his watch. Of course I chance for it as well as others. It takes place tomorrow... We now hear the raffle is to take place soon after dinner is done with. So it comes off at 4.30 p.m. after school hours. It causes an excitement among them all. After a great deal of high and low throwing poor Lewis's watch was won by a married man named Price.... I have a job on hand for Mr. Jones our 2nd mate. He wants me to raffle his panama hat. I could not refuse him so I managed to get 81 members at 3d. each and it's coming off after dinner."

A 'Judge and Jury' club was also formed towards the end of the voyage, with a judge, Queen's Councillors, usher of court, solicitors, constables etc. being elected from the passengers. "No doubt it will cause a great amusement amongst us if it's not put a stop to." The case lasted for over two hours. However two days later, "I find there is a stop put to our Judge and Jury Club, for it causes too much excitement. I must say they are the poorest lot I ever was with to get up any amusement."

Sunday morning was of course taken up with the Service which began at 10a.m. Everyone had to attend and it seemed as though the passengers preferred a lengthy sermon which would take up most of the morning for on Sunday "10th Dec. 10a.m. for Service and a married man named James is to officiate for the day which he does with a poor spirit by only reading a portion of scripture and reading church prayers. We hope to get a better one next Sunday. Its over by half past 11a.m." Two weeks later, "We then go below when we hear a new parson, a Mr. Ryan, and at the finish of reading prayers and singing a man gives us a fine extempour of words which sounds very pretty. It lasts about one and a half hours then dinner."

It would seem that this situation would have suited John Pickering very well, giving him much scope for his preaching abilities.

"Bell is now going for church. We all attend. It seems a change for us, if it's only going among the married ladies, it's some thing relieving and cheering to us. The word of God also does us some good, that takes the worldly thoughts from us for a time. In fact it's a pleasant few hours well spent."

Time was also spent observing nature at its best and worst. "I am highly pleased with the setting of the sun at sea. No landsman has any idea of the splendid scenes of nature at sea. It's beyond all description. Its magnificance.

"10a.m. there is now 12 ships in sight. See some of them quite plain. It's a fine sight for landsmen to see so many splendid ships in full sail and the heavenly scenes in the skys make the scene still lovelier. One of those ships now near us 11a.m. and crosses our bows. They are playing music on board and when she was near enough to us we fetched our music up on deck and played to them. The effect was grand and the sight was inspiring to all our dullards on board.

"After breakfast I strole on deck and was amused with many others in watching the dolphins darting about. It looks like a lump of gold in the water. One of our sailors tried to hook one only Mr. Dolphine was to artful for him.

"6.30 a.m. A great number of porpoises around the ship. I should say a thousand. Some appears the size of a sheep and smaller. They

25

caused a great attraction and amusement.

"We saw a great number of flying fish about 6.30 p.m. They are beautiful fish. Some are very small, some seem about a foot long, their wings are very fine like tissue paper".

"There was a large whale seen at 8a.m. in front of us on our starboard side. It spit a large spout of water into the air and it carried a surf of water for mile or more. It seemed miles off There are a great number of pilot fish seen following us. They are pretty fish. They look something like trout. It appears they are the pilot for the shark. They say when they are seen there is sure to be a shark near us.

"A great number of albatross birds are seen flying about. They are of a very large size. I have been told some measure 22ft. from tip to tip of wings and others are about the size of a wild duck. They have a very large beak, something like a goose. They are caught by a line with a piece of pork at the end of it. Some of us have caught one or two of them, it caused great amusement last evening by some of the passengers throwing at them pieces of biscuit and they would alight on the water like a duck and eat it. It caused a deal of amusement.

"16th Feb. A very large iceberg was seen early this morning on our port bows. It's to be plainly seen now. It appears by the naked eye about 40 or 60 feet high and about a quarter of a mile long and they tell me its 3 parts its depth in the water. A pretty little lump to knock up against a ship. I hear they always drift to windward and the man on the lookout can smell them a long distance off. They are beautiful things to look at."

The Doctor of course played a very important part on board ship. Two babies were born during the voyage and there were five deaths. There was also an outbreak of measles which filled the hospital, and at the start of the voyage a great deal of sea sickness, although this seemed to abate as the voyage got well under way.He was also required to extract the teeth of one of the sailors and was responsible for giving small pox vaccinations to those who needed them. Before every Sunday service he would take a roll call to see that no passengers were missing and to inspect to see that everyone was clean and decent. He also acted as peacemaker when frequent quarrels and fights erupted and seemed to issue all the law and order and serve punishments, usually stopping rations for the appropriate period. He also dealt with complaints of bad food and tried to reach an amicable conclusion.

"Our names is all called alphabetically to go to the Doctor to have your name and trade and age etc. entered in the book. I believe it's for the purpose of obtaining employment for them that wants it.

"4p.m. One of our young men in our mess is had before the Doctor with another from 41 mess for corresponding with the single girls. They are stopped rations for 24 hours, also the girl.

"9a.m. An order is now issued for all beds to be taken on deck for airing. Its a comic sight to see so many scores of chaps together with their beds spread out on the galleys and rails and sometimes when many are below and perhaps asleep it comes on to rain heavy then comes the amusement to see the scramble and slipping and sliding down, it's very amusing and then the Doctor is becalled for giving the orders to put them out. He is often in disgrace for many things. He must be a very funny doctor to be in favour of everyone."

A funeral at sea took place in the following manner:-

"10a.m. They are now preparing for the funeral of the little boy. It's a slight preparation.The body is sewn in canvas and placed on a board and slightly covers it with the Union Jack flag. It's then placed on the rail of the bulwarks and a seaman each side of it on the lee side of the ship. The Doctor reads the burial service, the Captain being present and at the words 'from life to death' the sailors tilt the board and it slides from under the flag into its ocean grave. It's a meloncoly sight, many shed tears."

Of course there was plenty of rough weather during the long voyage and some very bad storms. At the start of the passage, most passengers were very sea sick. "Nov 30th Doctor has just been below to turn all the sick ones out of their berths into the deck." Hardly had they reached the Bay of Biscay on "1st Dec.I have been very poorly this afternoon and so have dozens besides... .1 have not been bad five hours altogether for I resisted sea sickness by eating as much as I could directly after sick. It's a very good remedy against sea sickness. I am now tired and many being so sick. Among them some of our musicians so we are very quiet, and ship heaving slightly, we retire to rest about 8p.m." However, within a week or so, most passengers seemed to have got used to the rolling motion of the ship and conquered their sea sickness.

When the storms came, they came in force and whilst in the North Atlantic "we again had a very stormy rolling night, I was awake out of my sleep by pails and cooking utensils in our compartment breaking away from their moorings. Many of the Irish boys thought she would become a wreck. It continued rolling till half past 11a.m. when we found it a difficulty to venture up on deck for our coffee.... So severe was the morning that scores was calling on the Lord to save them and many other such observations and at the same time the sailors were cursing the ship."

A week later, "1p.m. a heavy gale of wind is arose while at dinner when we hear a terrific noise up on deck. A panic arises momentary when all the frightened boys rushes on deck and leaves their dinner. When we found of our fore topmast stunsail boom broke and nearly carried one of the sailors overboard. Many lost their dinners through leaving it which caused a bother. I hope they will get use to it by and by."

Christmas Eve and another storm. "Ship has been rolling very all day and night and all our pots and kettles flying about the deck. At 37 Mess when they had brought their duff from the oven, it flew into the middle of the deck to the fun of many of us."

After a fairly calm period on "31st Jan. Awoke this morning but not very refreshed from my nights rest for she was rolling and pitching heavily all night which disturbed me greatly and the awful noise from the tin pots and plates dashing about and pails breaking away from their moorings.. One of my mates lost his hot coffee now through the ship rolling so we all had to subscribe a trifle to his empty cup for him to make up a breakfast. 10a.m. A scene in the married department. The women and children tumbling over each other and the crashing of pots and pans over their heads and the capsizing of sundry articles such as pickles and mustard tea etc." The following day, "She is still rolling about worse than she did in the Bay of Biscay. She gave a fearful lurch last night. My hammock nearly touched the deck. It must have been awful sensation for those that sleep in berths. I would prefer a hammock to a berth any time".

"17th Feb. Some amusement happens on deck after dinner by the washers up of plates and souptins for a very heavy sea comes over the ship and throws men, boys, tin pots and plates all about the deck in the manner of speaking. One brother could scarcely recognise the other as to whose utensils they were. It took a long time to sort them out, for that was an opportunity for those messes who were short of mugs or plates to replenish their stock. It caused many a bother and nearly a fight about many tins."

"25th Feb. the wind is blowing a terrific gale from N.N.W. It shivers the very masts in her. All the hatchways is battened down except ours and that is partly except a little hole to creep through. I remain on deck the most part of the storm till I went down to dinner, but it was a job to eat it after the difficult work of fetching it from the galley, particular the soup. We went through a regular gymnastic dinner. It was a regular catch and bite for it and when dinner was over then came the tumbles over each other. Two or three chaps were completely thrown under the tables and one cut his eye very badly to get a sure footing. Many chaps sit down on the deck and have a slide for it."

The Captain had made the decision to sail through the Bass Strait, thereby reducing the length of the journey. He had never taken this route before, but as the weather was fair, he had calculated to sail most of the distance in daylight. What followed would be indelibly etched on the minds of all the passengers for the rest of their lives. It is left to the remarkable eye witness account to give details of this daunting experience. "7th March. Awoke very early this morning by the sweet cry of land in sight which many did not believe for they thought it was only a hoax but when I got on deck I saw an immense track of land. It was Cape Otway, the entrance of Bass Straight and it being a fine clear morning and calm. It made the sight still beautiful. It was within six miles of us and we still drew nearer till the wind got to much a head of us and we was obliged to tack ship. On the point of this land Cape Otway is a lighthouse and a flag pole by which we signalled her and said who we were and where bound for. There is a telegraph there, so in a few minutes they were made acquainted of our coming, both in Sydney and Melbourne. The scene was very enlivening and exciting to hundreds of us for its months since we seen land before, for the last we seen was Canary Islands. It put a new heart in scores of the passengers. 11a.m. We are now in Bass Straight which is I believe about 700 miles from Sydney. We are scarcely moving. I do hope a breeze

will soon spring up. "We have still an head wind against us but at
4p.m. it changes all of a sudden for a straight fair course through
the dangerous straights. It's now increasing to a gale. We now take
in our mizzen topsails... .6.0 p.m. Wind is much stronger, it pleases
us all. This beautiful stiff fair breeze. I hear we are now about 80
miles from Cape Wilson and the light house It appears this place is
one of the most dangerous places in my idea in the world for it's a
passage between two immense rocks with numerous other large
rocks surrounding it. It is only about one mile wide. It's a great
terror to all shipping is passing through this Cape Wilson. We are
now going a great speed and our Captain wishes to pass through
this place at daylight if he can. If he don't find he can pass it before
it gets dark which it is fast approaching, he says he will have the
ship hove too in the wind which we all hope he will not have to do.
The meaning of the ship being hove too is to brace the fore and
main yards and topsails on them contrary way to the wind by so
doing the ship although in heavy gale of wind fair course is
completely stopped and so turned that the wind blows over her
quarter and then she is completely to the mercy of the seas. There is
no danger of heaving a ship too in the open seas for there is plenty
of sea room but here in this straights which is over 300 miles long
is swarmed with sunken rocks and some of them only 10 feet below
the surface of the sea and to the leeward of us is mighty rocks so
thus describing our position and dangers we are very fast approaching.

"I will proceed to give you as near a description as possible I can
being an eye witness to all I am about to describe to you. At half
past six she was going at such speed we never before seen her go 15
knots an hour and still increasing in her speed and wind. 8p.m. the
wind is now getting to a terrific heights. We take in all her royals
and lower topsails. I hear the Captain now say he will not be able to

31

pass the Cape Wilson before dark and to venture it, it would be to
the sacrifice of nearly 500 lives and the ship and also our Captain
not having ever passed through these straights before, places us all
in a queer predicament. I hear him now order both watches aloft, to
shorten immediately sail, stop the ship's way for she is fast flying
into danger. They are now shortening her sail very fast. We have 31
sailors aloft and on deck. It's fast getting dark and all the passengers are now very terrified.

"It's now blowing nearly a hurricane and dashing all things
asunder, ropes and casks etc. We are advised to go below but I
remain with three others of my mess on deck under the poop where
I was nearly fastened for safety. We have now only her fore main
and mizzen topsails up and as they are furling her inner gib, it blow
to ribbons as did her halliards. Many of the sailors remarked it is
the heaviest gale of wind they have seen for some time. I never
beheld such a sight, as many other say in their lives."

The Captain, finding she is still making too much way he orders
her mizzen topsails to be close reefed for he said if he could get her
down to 5 knots an hour he would venture to pass through them
tonight, but at this speed it is terrific we are safe to go to destruction
if he does. She has now only two sails on her, that's her fore and
main upper topsails and the storm is so great that we are going
almost at the same speed. I am happy to say it did not rain if it did
I could not tell you the awful consequences for the ropes would
have been wet for working.

"There is now great excitement and talk between the Captain and
officers and at half past eleven p.m. we were put the ship and hove
her too then come the awful scene for the wind had reached to such
an height that every timber in her trembled under your feet. I have
before described to you the manner they hove her too. She appeared
quite locked in the sea and we were entirely to the mercy of the

raging waves which were rolling mountains high and the awful howling winds.... All of a sudden her lower fore topsail gets unfurled and blows away to atoms into the sea and soon after away goes her main upper topsail and trembled the huge mighty masts as they went. And now smash goes the skylight over the single girls' place and then comes the awful screeches and wailings and rushes up stairs. They had to be locked down or they would have been dashed overboard. Then all the married people and single men were at prayers as well as the girls.

"Ship only having one sail on her that was her main upper topsail. In another instant a fearful gale comes and rips that sail down the middle and blows the one end to ribbons and the other end to the yard which saved our lives for had that of blown away she would of rolled and plunged herself under and drowned herself As it was the Lord's hand was upon us in mercy. Now most part of her halliards and rigging were being torn away by the awful winds and the noise of her tattered sails and ropes were in sound similar to artillery going off and the heavy seas were dashing over her.

"All the scene was too horrible to describe to you".

"The ship now appears a mear skeleton without sail and almost ropes. She is now what they call under bare poles except that fortunate piece of topsail which kept her head up a little. Everyone now seems in an awful state of excitement and confusion even the Captain and his officers looks in terror of their awful position for we are fast going to leeward on the rocks. Everything is smashing and tearing away.

"About 2a.m. when the hurricane was at its height and nearly all hope banished, I seen the carpenter come on deck with his axe and plumb lead for sounding depths of water. This sight I must say I was aroused with the awful fear of she soon becoming wrecked for I fancy I heard the Captain say cut the mast down. But I suppose it was the awful feeling I then felt.

"The bold Captain and crew which in all amounted 40 were perfectly useless for they could not go aloft nor set sail for such was the state of the wind. I heard him say once or twice, I wish it was daylight. We all were awaiting the awful doom that we thought were awaiting every soul on board. All were in ernest prayer and I truly asked of the Almighty to direct our course to a safe landing and also to strengthen our noble Captain and his gallant crew and be an instrument in their hands for our preservation. Every soul of us appeared perfectly resigned to the fate before us also the girls they were in swoons and in ernest prayer in their apartment."

"At 3a.m. the Engineer come on deck by orders and was trying to get steam up in case she sprung a leak, to work the steam pumps to pump her out but he could not do it. Sea was running too high and the great gale was too boisterous and she roiling down to her waters edge and tremendous seas dashing over her. It was out of his power to work the engine, it was shifted by dashing seas. I often enquired how far the rocks were off and I was told they could see the breakers at a slight distance of about one and half miles.

"Everyone was now asked if they had made their peace with God, if not to do so at once.

"While the lovely moon was now coming from under a dense cloud and showing us light in our awful troubles and the splendid rays of blue clouds were to be seen over us indication to us our Gods great power of quietening the mighty seas and winds. We then seen on our starboard side another small bark in great distress, scarcely a sail or rope on her and her bulwarks stove in by the awful seas, but God's hand was still over us poor souls and she was kept from dashing against us. It terrified our mate and Captain when he first seen it, but thank God we rolled away more from her till we left her some long way behind us. I hear she lost three poor sailors washed

over. The winds and seas were quite as rough as ever only those clouds indicated to us the awful storm would soon abate. I then at half past 3 a.m. managed by crawling and holding onto, cross the bewildered deck which was strewed with an immense amount of broken spars and ropes and broken casks etc. To go below were another awful sight came before me such as I never wish again to see. All our place was a complete wreck. Our tables partly broken. All our utensils and tinware I may say hundreds of pots, cups, plates, buckets and bowls lay strewn all over the ground. Men and boys fell out of their hammocks in fright while others were on their faces on the ground in prayers and lying over the tables and in fact the sight was too horrible to pen to you.

"All over the ship was one wreck and ruin, and myself being greatly terrified from fright and being benumbed for I was never off the deck from half past six p.m. till half past three a.m. I felt dreadfully cold. I had a little brandy left in my flask and I drank it and it revived me greatly and I suddenly dropped off to sleep on one of the tables, being overdone, never troubling whether she went down or not. I then awoke again in a very few minutes and went on deck when I found to my great delight that daylight was fast approaching and the Captain at a quarter to four a.m. gave orders to put her before the wind and she was put about, and thanks to the Almighty we were once more going on our fair course in safe waters. Although she had gone a great distance out of her course she had only this lucky half a main topsail on for I heard for a fact that if the whole of that sail had of blown away we should have gone to destruction for the ship would have drowned herself by rolling and plunging about for she would have had nothing to of kept her head up. We are now on a safe rout at 10 knots an hour with great thanks to the Almighty for his preservation.

"8th March 4a.m. Great noise and bustle is still going on and confusion seems to surround us for on deck and between decks there is nothing but wreck and disorder. We do not get our days allowance of water served out at 6a.m. The voice of the steward calling out the numbers of different messes seems to refreshen every soul of them as it was a true sign all was safe. Then comes the search for lost and strayed property. Some had lost their boots and their trousers and even their shirts and scarves or stockings and after a time of bustle and labour every man got sufficiently dressed in his or anyone elses clothes and then come to find his bed clothes which was all in parts of the ship. And they now tie their hammocks up and stow it away and now its near breakfast time.

"The different messes now got the puzzling job to search for their pots and mugs, teapots, butter etc. I assure you it was a very laughable scene to see the different mixtures at some tables such as tea caddy upset into the molasses pot and the mustard turned into the butter. And in fact everything was amalgamated together and scores of pots and plates, knives and forks were broken, bent and lost. It took hours before it was all cleared away.

"I then went on deck where I blessed myself to see such a destructive scene. I could scarcely walk the deck for loads of broken sails and ropes and spars that strewed the decks and scores of pale looking wild dismayed passengers looking around them wondering where they were for all her rigging and halliards were in all disorder and great talk is going on in groups about the great deliverance and God's great mercy to us through this great storm.

"Some preparations are now being made for clearing the decks. I then took a glance into our galleys, well I could not help smiling to see all the pots and kettles turned over and it appears today is fresh bread day and last night the baker had set the sponge for today's

baking and that was sent all over the bakehouse and the pots embedded into it. In fact everything was in disorder. As regards the single girls, I cannot say much about them but I hear a great many met with various accidents and other distresses. The married people the same, for one married man was pitched right into the middle of the deck and the same loss and breakage as us. Our breakfast cannot be got ready yet for they have not lit the fires.

"Half past 8a.m. A cry of land is heard from the man on lookout and I found it is those horrid looking rocks and gastly Islands that we were afraid of going through last night. We are fast approaching them and I only wish it had been light enough to of passed through them yesterday. It would of made 200 miles different to us by now, but yet I must be very thankful its no worse. She is now going 10 knots an hour with a good fair breeze from S.S.W. the same quarter as last nights gale.

"9.0 a.m. We are now passing Cape Wilson and those mighty rocks. They are massive in appearance and very high. In my opinion if a ship were to strike them there would be no chance of saving a soul as the seas dash so high up them. I only regret I am no hand at sketching or 1 would give you a drawing. We now pass them through in perfect safety thanks to the Almighty for his preservation to us.

"Orders is now given for all woodwork to be thoroughly washed and cleaned today in readiness for quarantine where we shall be inspected by colonial inspectors. I expect it will be nothing else but scrubbing and washing now till we get to quarantine.

"We are now still sailing as usual on an average of nine and a half knots all day on a fair course. We are steering N.E. by E. and the wind is now S.W. by S. We all seem very quietly and I feel sleepy. Wind is now fast decreasing. I expect we shall have a calm after wind goes down. We soon retire to rest at 8p.m. being almost exhausted me in particular.

"God grant us peace tonight".

The journey took approximately three and a half months, and varied enormously in speed from day to day. After five weeks they had reached the Canary Islands, and on 26th December, Boxing Day, "Very fast wind same course. Ship rolls very much, she is making good headway at 9 knots an hour. That's 216 miles a day or 1512 a week.... It causes many smiling faces among the passengers. Even the Captain is cheered up by this change for we have had some much head winds against us since we have been out. We do more in 3 or 4 days now than we did in a month before."

From then to the end of the voyage mileage varied from as little as 30 miles in 24 hours when they were becalmed, to as much as 253 miles in the same period.

During the voyage the passengers had experienced the dawning of the New Year. "I heard it whispered just now that it's the navel practice at sea to drum the old year out and new one in. There is only a few passengers know it, so I waited up while all the others were asleep. When 8 bells strike (12 o'clock) then commenced the spree. All the sailors of both watches (port and starboard) comes out with pots and kettles and beats empty casks and sound the large bell. It was one of the awfulest noises I ever heard in my life. It was too terrible to describe. The Captain came out in a fright thinking the ship was afire and cursing the men for not fixing the hose along the ship. As usual it was forgot that night worst luck then first mait came and soon put a stop to it. I thought it would have terminated with heavy work for to see the men rushing up stairs in their shirts by dozens. I laughed to such an extent it nearly made me bad. After a short time all was quiet and they all returned to their beds on the beginning of another year and I hope a happy and prosperous one for us all."

Crossing the line caused great curiosity: "Orders is just post up by the Captains Orders that no shaving is to be practised while crossing the equator. I hold with the order its proper. It will save many a bother for there are some rough chaps here. Sailors can do as they like to themselves. There are dozens of men anxiously looking forward to crossing the line. Its laughable to hear the different opinions of them all as to the meaning of the line. Some of the sailors trys to persuade them many silly meanings, some believe it.

"There are now much talk about crossing the line. I expect we shall cross it about breakfast time tomorrow. The sailors declare they will have a lark with some of us. I know they wont with me, I shall keep out of the way.

"Saturday morning. Up early and many enquiries to know if we have crossed the line. None of their minds or wishes were satisfied until her latitude was put up when we found out she crossed it at 9.30 a.m. to the satisfaction of everyone of the passengers. The sailors were all quiet but their hands were itching to have some fun. "The sailors are now having a spree on the forecastle. They are shaving each other and two or three passengers were caught after dark and tarred. They had no right to be among them. All the crew were done they looked like wild Indians. They were soon washed and in the bunks (beds) and all was soon quiet."

During the long enforced closeness one with another, they would all have experienced a variety of emotions, some good, some bad, which would have made them into different, more experienced people. In our eye witness's words, "Emigration makes any single chap a useful, domesticated member of society in sewing and mending, washing, cooking and chamber work".

John, and Sarah and Joseph John, at the end of their safe passages, sharing similar experiences at sea, would have been able to meet the challenges of a new life with greater fortitude and flexibility, thanking Almighty God for giving them the chance to make the very best of all the opportunities opened up to them.

Chapter 3

From information received from the Shipping Lists Passenger Arrivals in South Australia, John Pickering arrived on 11 May, 1849 but the actual point of landing differs between two sources of information - one suggests the port of entry as Holdfast Bay, the other Port Adelaide.

We can only guess at his thoughts when setting foot on dry land, but the relief of surviving the long, hazardous journey would overwhelm him.

Passengers were allowed half a ton of baggage, together with their livestock, which included cows, pigs, and fowls. There is no record of John taking anything with him, but we do know from his letters that he landed "with 1/8d. in my pocket" - a proud boast when he looked back at what he had achieved.

On arrival his name was John Pickering, not John Pickerill as shown on his baptismal entry and Marriage Certificate. The reason can only be puzzled over. Did the person recording his entry when boarding ship not hear correctly, or could he not understand the accent? Did he know that his grandfather Christopher was also known as Christopher Pickering as well as Pickrell? The surname Pickering is more common than Pickerill, so did he think to himself new country - new life - new name?

The South Australian Primitive Methodist Record of July 1885 states, "For a short time he settled in Norwood, and then removed to Salisbury, and became the staff and stay of our cause in the place." However, he could not have stayed in Norwood for long, because in 1849 he is recorded as burying land in Salisbury.

On 11 August, 1847 John Harvey had gained a Land Grant from Governor Robe, and obtained 172 acres of land in Sections 2191 and 2230, and this marked the beginning of a township. He had a town plan drawn up and divided into lots. By June 1848 he was selling this land and decided to call the town Salisbury after the county town of his wife's English home county of Wiltshire. He had paid around £1.0s.0d. for each acre.

This sale of land must have come to the attention of John, who purchased in 1849:-

Plot No 69 for £12.0s.0d; Plot No.53 for £10.0s.0d; Plots Nos.75 and 76 for £16.0s.0d. and Plot No.16 for £5 0s 0d.

An early brick kiln in Salisbury, possibly the Pickering and Miller works

Plots 53/75/76 were purchased by Pickering and Miller for a brick-works, the first in Salisbury. It is presumed that Joseph Bass Miller was his business partner, but it is not known whether it was an actual legal partnership. Was Joseph Bass Miller already known to John?

Could they have sailed together on the 'Stebonheath' with the purpose of establishing a brick-works? John must have had prior knowledge of the area in which he wanted to settle, as the ground had to contain clay for the making of bricks. Was this information given to him before he set sail?

Plot 16 was bought with the intention of building a Primitive Methodist Chapel and plots 69 and 53 were almost opposite each other in Ann Street, as is stated in John Harvey's own records contained in *I Called It Salisbury* by A.P. Harvey.

Extract from John Harvey's Register of Land Sales for Salisbury 1849, clearly showing that John had bought Plot 16 expressly for the building of a chapel

It is also recorded in H. John Lewis's book *Salisbury, A History of Town and District,* that 'the trustees were Joseph Kinsey, wheel-wright, Michael Marra, farmer, Benjamin Green, farmer and Joseph Miller, brickmaker, which could indicate that Joseph Miller was a fellow Primitive Methodist. However, there is no mention of John Pickering. Is the record about to be 'set straight'?

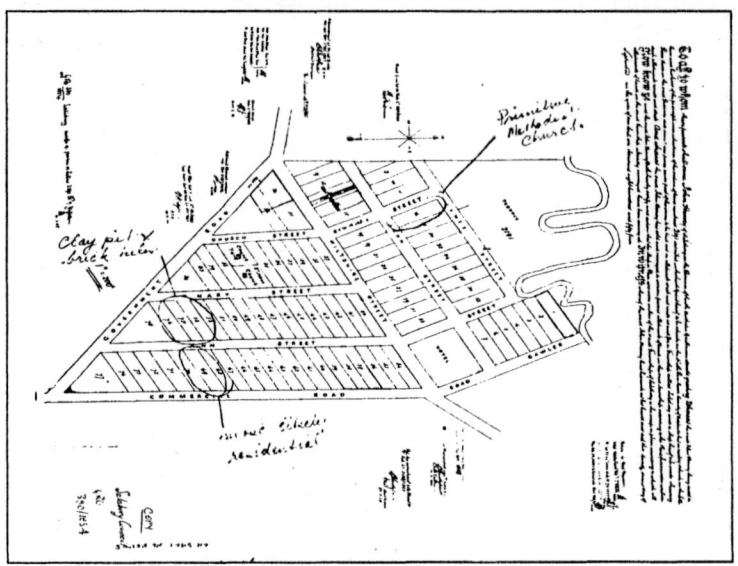

John Harvey's plan of Salisbury showing the locations of the brick-making enterprise, John Pickering's residence and the Primitive Methodist Church

Meanwhile, in July 1853 John was busy buying another plot of land in Salisbury, No.54, sandwiched between Wiltshire Street, Ann Street and Commercial Road. He bought this land from Thomas Wright for £30.0s.0d. (Land Registry Memorial 65/63) Perhaps he bought this land as an investment, because in April 1854 he sold it to Daniel Brady, farmer, for £103.0s.0d (Land Registry Memorial 448/70) making a healthy profit.

On 23 July 1853, having lived in Salisbury for over four years. he writes the following letter to his father in Cannock, England

Salisbury July 23:1853

Dear and Honoured parent;
I write to you hoping to find you in good health as it leaves me at this time through God's mercy with thankfulness I can say I never enjoyed a better state of health so that I am able to go through my labour with pleasure, but I am not so happy as I wish to be, the delay of my wife and child adds greatly to my sorrows, although I thought I had made every necessary requirement to get her out, but the agent of the Family Colonisation Society kept back part of the money which I paid into the Society and that is the cause of the delay I was very much affected when I received the last letter from my wife informing me of the case. The letter was 6 months in reaching to me, the steamer was detained on her passage for want of fuel which made her so long. As soon as I received the letter I went to Adelaide, but could not find the man that I paid the passage to, I thought it the best way to send her money to pay her passage herself I sent a registered letter with a draft on the Bank for £40

45

and I enclose another in this. if she has not received it please to send her this as soon as you can possibly. After I had sent for my wife last May twelve months, I made preparations to return to the diggings, and after purchasing 8 bullocks and dray and a load of bacon, butter and flour, we set off overland a 500 mile journey and was 6 weeks and 3 days in getting to the Goldfields. When I arrived there I was troubled, expecting the arrival of my family, I could not stay long for it would be very hard for her to come and not find me there. I bought a light dray and brought back two of the bullocks and came to Salisbury again, leaving my mate to sell the load and the 6 bullocks and dray. On my return back, if had time, I tell you of the poor natives of the Bush, without a stitch of clothing upon them, how they come to the drays to beg damper, their customs and manner is very strange, they know nothing of the God that made them.

I was 3 weeks and three days in coming back and since then I have been at the Brickyard again. We are doing very well in our business with the brickwork and the lime trade. I should like to hear a little oftener from you, the letters from you resemble angels visits few and far between. With thankfulness I inform you that I am still living for heaven. I hold the office of an unworthy minister in our beloved connection, the Society is doing well and we are living at peace. The chapel that I built is now too small, we intend enlarging this summer, there is a nice Sunday School in it doing well.

Dear Father, I don't ever expect to see your face again in the flesh, but I hope to see you in heaven, but if we have not living for heaven, we shall not get there. Heaven is a holy place, its inhabitants are holy, and it is said in the Book of God, without holiness no man shall see God. Dear Father, do not neglect to seek the one thing needful. I often think of you with deep sorrow when think how you used to go to the gardening on Sunday, and after the rent,

doing contrary to God's will when he has said 'remember the Sabbath Day to keep it holy'. Do bear these things in mind and may God bless you.
Give my love to my dear Mother, and all my brothers and sisters. Please give my Christian affection to my Bretheren at Hednesford, and Pogey Lane. I conclude my epistle to you my dear Father, and remain your affectionate Son

John Pickering
Salisbury,
South Australia

Wife and child? Records searched to date suggest that when John left for South Australia there were no children by this marriage, which had taken place eighteen months before setting out. There is no date of sailing but he arrived in South Australia on 11 May, 1849, therefore he might well have set sail in the middle to end of February, 1849. The timing here is crucial, as Sarah gave birth to a son on 19 October, 1849, and although that date has not been given on any official records, it appears in a Family Register, possibly at the front of the family bible, and is still in the possession of the Pickering family. It is known for certain that Joseph John, son of John and Sarah Pickering, was baptised at Golds Green Primitive Methodist Church, in the parish of West Bromwich, on 2 December, 1849, the ceremony performed by S. Sanders, who could have been one of Sarah's relations. It is interesting here to note that the surname given was Pickering and not Pickerill.

We can only imagine Sarah's feelings at the prospect of mother-hood with no one to give her financial support. There was no welfare state, maternity benefit or child benefit to rely on and where she lived is not known, although it is possible that she lived with her father, and family legend tells us that she and her mother kept a small shop, but what is certain is that Sarah took a very long lime to make the final decision to join her husband.

In total, John sent her £80.0s.0d plus the money he had paid into the Family Colonisation Society - quite a substantial amount in 1853. The National Colonisation Society had been founded by Edward Gibbon Wakefield and Robert Gouger who believed that land in the colony was to be sold at a fixed minimum price and strictly regulated to prevent the disorganisation in South Australia which had occurred in New South Wales. Proceeds from the land sales would be used primarily to assist the passage of bone fide immigrants who were carefully selected to ensure they were respectable, of good character, energetic, and also create the right balance of ages and sexes.

Did Sarah use the money on which to live, seeing it as her due, or did John send her regular amounts to support her and their son while they were apart?

The gold rush had started after John had set up home in Salisbury, and it appears that in 1853 he had made at least two journeys to the goldfields. These journeys were long and arduous, particularly if the only means of transport was by foot. Swamps had to be negotiated and the track was not well marked, particularly in winter when it was overgrown. However for those who went in groups or could afford a dray and bullock team, the journey was somewhat easier although mosquitoes and sand flies were an irritant.

Not all the diggers at the goldfields were successful, and some, flushed with success, quickly spent their fortunes on 'wine, women and song'. Others who were more prudent could do very well, and could deposit in the bank maybe £1000 for just a few weeks' work. The biggest nugget ever found, a few inches below the surface, weighed over 200 lbs. and was sold for £9,500.

There is no indication that John and his mate found gold, although he could have written earlier letters than the ones found, but I am sure he would have mentioned any good fortune at some point in his correspondence.

In December 1853, John's name, and that of his partner Joseph Miller, together with most of the other residents of Salisbury, appear on a petition to His Excellency Sir Henry Edward Fox Young, Knight Lieutenant Governor of the Province of South Australia, requesting that "Mr. James Jepson, Storekeeper in the said township" be appointed Postmaster for Salisbury, in preference to the already appointed Mr. McCabe.

Their objections were that Mr McCabe was a perfect stranger to them having only just arrived in the township, and that the premises intended to be used as the Post Office was a mere slab hut, in very bad repair and totally unfit for the safe custody of the mails. In addition a serious objection arose from the position of the intended office, at the bottom of a steep hill and most inconvenient, if not dangerous for carriages to pull up at whereas Mr. Jepson's general store, in the very centre of Salisbury was a substantial stone and brick building and had convenient access from all sides. It was also considered by the petitioners to be 'more eligible' for the safe custody and convenient distribution of the mails.

The mail would be the most important method of communication between isolated communities and the petitioners would be keen to safeguard this facility. The tone of the several letters back and forth suggests that this facility had been withdrawn for some time past from Little Para to Salisbury. The Colonial Secretary intended to restore the link and had received tenders from Mr. McCabe who offered to conduct the Post Office and carry the mail for £15 per annum, and an anonymous one to convey the mail alone for £55 per annum.

49

of course Mr. McCabe's tender was accepted, but he would be replaced if he proved to be unsatisfactory.

It is obvious that by this time John Pickering and Joseph Miller, as listed petitioners, were very much part of the Salisbury community.

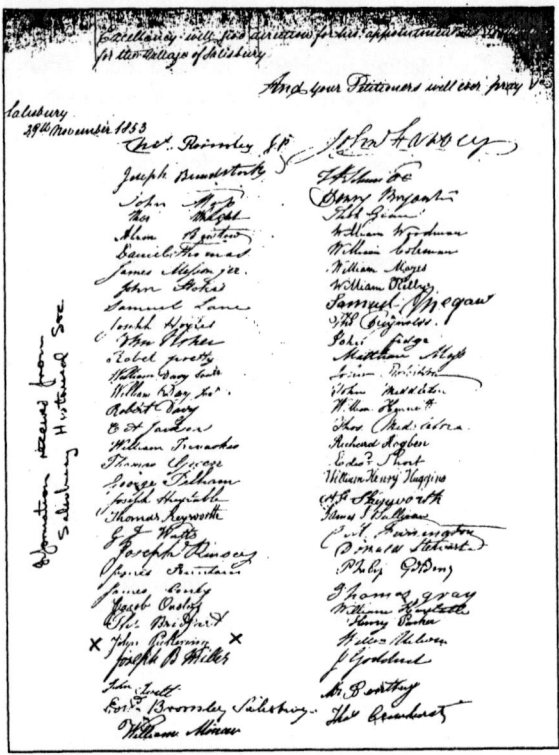

The signatories of the 'Humble Petition of the... inhabitants of Salisbury and vicinity concerning the Postal Service, including those of Pickering and Miller

50

Salisbury Jan 19 1854

Dear and Honoured Parent,
I write to you hoping to find you and all the family in a good state
of health as it leaves me at present I can still praise God for his
goodness to me, notwithstanding I am very uncomfortable in my
mind very much dissatisfied about my wife and child. I have
received a letter from her stating that she cannot come for want of
more money She informed me when disappointed by Mrs Chisl-
ham(sic) Society that she should draw the £30 and bank it until I
could send some more, as soon that I knew I sent £40 more,
sufficient to bring them out, now she informs me that she is wanting
more. I have made another trial and if she does not come this
fourth time, I shall not try any more, nor send her any more, I shall
entirely give her up for good I did not leave my home to move into
a far country for a mere living I could have got that in England I
want something for old age, if I should want it, I have done well
considering how I have been situated if I had my wife with me I
should have been worth £200 more by this time. I have agreed with
the Government this time to bring my family out and sent Sarah an
order to send to the Emigration Commissioner, and there is nothing
for them to pay. I have paid the passage and if they do not come I
shall have the money returned. I think sometimes I shall be able to
return back about the year of 1860 If things continue favourable,
when I have got £1500 I shall come back I have money and
property now worth from £400 to £500 and my business is turning
me in a pound a day. If my wife comes, I have sent for a pug mill,
the spindle is the chief thing and
I have also paid the passage for Joseph if he likes to come, and I
will give him 2 guineas a week to come and drive my dray. The men
in the Brickyard are getting 8 shillings a day. Bricks are selling at

1854

Salisbury Jen 19.

Dear and Honoured Parent i write to you hoping to
find you and all the family in a good state of health
as itt leavs mee att presant i can still praise God for
his Goodness to mee notwithstanding i am very
uncomfortable in my mind very much Desatis
fied about my wife and child i have received a
letter from her stating that shee can nott come
for want of more money shee informed mee
when Disapointed by Mrs Chidham Society
thatt shee should draw the 30 £ and Bank off
untill i could send some more as soon that i knew
i sent 40 £ more suffiecent to bring them out
now shee informs mee that shee is wanting more
i have made a nother treal and if shee dont nott
come this forth time i shall not try aney mor
nor send to her aney more i shall entirely give
her up for good i did nott leave my home to rove
into a fer cuntry for a meer living i could have
gott that in England i want something for old age iff
i should want itt i have done well considering
how i have been situated if i'd my wife with mee
i should have been worth 200 £ more by this time

52

i have agreed with the Goverment thiss time
to bring my family out and sent Sarah a order
to send to the Emegration Comissioner and there
is nothing for them to pay i have payed the pas=
and if thay doe nott come i shall have the money
returned i think sometimes i shall bee able to
return back about the year of 1860 if things
continue favourable when i have gott 1500£
i shall come back i have money and property
now worth from 4 to 500£ and my Bissness
is turning mee in a pound Daly if my Wife
comes i have sent for Peggness the spindle
is the cheef thing and i have also paid the
passage for Joseph if hee like to come and i
will give him 2 Guinies a week to come and
drive my Dray the men in the Brickyard
are getten 8 shillings a Day Bricks are selling
att the Kiln att 4£ a 1000 I should feel abliged
to you to answer thiss letter giving mee the
pertecklers of things for i so seldom here i
you give my Love to all the family and enquir
frends and i Conclud for it is time to bee in Bed
and remain your Affectionate Sun Jam Pickering
    take care of your Sole

the kiln at £4. 0s. 0d a 100cwt.

I should feel obliged to you to answer this letter giving me the particulars of things, for I so seldom hear about you, give my love to all the family and enquiring friends, and I conclude for it is time to be in bed, and remain your affectionate son.

John Pickering

Take care of your soul

Mrs. Caroline Chisholm, wife of Captain Archibald Chisholm, with her charitable zeal and energy, realised there was a need for advice to be given to new arrivals, particularly the unprotected position of female and often friendless emigrants as well as to help emigrants who desired to pay the passage of the families. She is the person referred to in the letter. The pugrnill that John asked for was probably invented by the Dutch in the seventeenth century and was a vertical tube of wood or iron with a shaft from which projects a spiral of horizontal knives. A horse, harnessed to the end of a long beam joined to the shaft head, circles the mill. Clay is fed into the top, kneaded by the knives and extruded from the bottom. Children were often employed to carry or barrow the clay to the moulding bench. This piece of equipment would probably have been made in one of the numerous factories which existed in the Black Country at that time, and near to where Sarah's father resided.

Dear and Honoured Parent,

I again take the opportunity of sending a few lines to you believing you will be glad to receive them from your unworthy son. I am thankful to God my heavenly father for all the blessings I enjoy both temporal and spiritual and although in a distant land above 16,000 miles from my native land I do still love the Lord and feel him precious to my soul

The little chapel that we built in Salisbury we have enlarged it, we have expended about £200 and at the re-opening services, the collections amounted to £117. 0s. 0d. The chapel is well filled, I preached in it last Sunday and we are going to build another about four miles from me. I am expecting a missionary out to live in Salisbury, I hope he will be one of the right sort, this is a horrid sinful colony I believe the devil will have his part of souls out of these colonies. Religion is at a very low ebb, it is almost become a form with the power. I praise God my face is still sunwards and by his grace I hope to see him face to face without a cloud between. I hope, dear father, you have found him of whom Moses and the prophets spoke of for it is a fearful thing to fall into the hands of the living God. You remember we are to strive to enter in at the silver gate.

I never hear anything about brother Thomas, how he is doing and how he spends his time, I hope he is not living in the habitual dirty state that he was the last time I saw him. I often think of the poor working man with you, and contrast them with the labouring man here, I am giving ten shillings per day to labouring men and £1.5s. per 1000 for making bricks. Trade is good here, Carpenters are getting 17s 0d per day, Bricklayers the same, there is great demand for building material land is got up in price. I sold half an acre of land in Salisbury for £103 - I gave £30 for it. I sold a few days ago,

40 acres for £160 - I gave £100 for it, and I think to start another Brickyard and apply my money in my business, for I think it will pay me better, if things go on as they have for three more years, I shall be in easy circumstances. I think now, that I have got in stock and money £700, and when I can land in England with £1500 I shall come home. I never intend to come back to work for a master I wish there would come a odstuff maker out, I could find one a good job, there is no tiles made in the colony but what I make. I want a pugmill, I sent word for my wife to bring one with her. I have not heard from her yet in answer to the order that I sent dated 4th January, so that I do not know whether she will come or not I did not send her any money but I paid the money into Government Treasury for her and the lad, her father, and Joseph, and if they do not come, I shall receive the sum back I think if she had tried, she might have come with the amount that I sent, if she does not come, I do not intend to send an more for I may send all I have and be no forwarder, if she does not bring a pug mill with her, will you get me one made. I only want the iron work, the spindle to be 6ft 6" long and 12 knives, you can write to some of the shipping agents at London to get it on board a ship, and they will let you know when and how to send it and the expences of the freight; then send me word by letter and I will send you the money back. I should like to hear from you a little oftener and send the news of the place.

I have just set my potatoes, peas, turnips, the onions are up, cabbage look well, but a very dry time like the first winter I came here, crops look very bad, particularly on the plains, the hills are better.

Please give my kind love to the bretheren at Hednesford, I rejoice to see the account of the chapel in the magazines, also to the bretheren at Pogey Lane, I hope the Lord is saving souls at Booth Place. Remember me to all my brothers and sisters and mother, say in your next letter whether sister Elizabeth is married or likely to be, and to whom, his abilities and character and occupation or calling. I shall write again as soon as I hear how it will be with me, so I conclude with my kindest regards to you my dear parent and remain your humble but affectionate son,

> *John Pickering*
> *Brickmaker,*
> *Salisbury.*

Aug 7 1854

Please answer as soon as possible.

The little chapel in Salisbury seems to be very central in John's life at this particular time, and he was obviously a lay preacher as is illustrated by his comments in his letter. On 23 September 1854 the trustees took possession of land donated by Thomas Smith for a primitive Methodist Chapel to be built at Burton, approximately four miles west of Salisbury. It was completed in 1858 and provided a worship centre for the farmers who had settled in the area. The trustees listed were: Joseph Kinsey, John Pickering, James Dredge, Rewell Bentley, John Bradshaw, William Diment, Henry Bryant and Thomas Abbott. From 1860 it also served as a school and continued to do so up until July 1950, and up until 1900 would have had a larger membership than Salisbury. The Salisbury Circuit was established in December 1857 and the Burton church was included in its five churches, and the total membership for the circuit was 50. The letter also states that he is 'expecting a missionary', and it is speculation as to whether it would be John Gibbon Wright who eventually became known as Father Wright and did much to promote by 1900 the union of the Wesleyans, Bible Christians and the Primitive Methodists. He arrived in South Australia in January 1856 and spent the first three years at Burra, a hundred miles north of Adelaide, and within three years was appointed President of the South Australian Conference. Further evidence suggests that this man was highly regarded by the Pickering family, becoming very well known to them.

The wages that John was paying his men provide an interesting comparison to wages in England at that time. The rate for a labourer was 10s.0d. per day, with tradesmen earning 17s.0d per day. The wage for making 1000 bricks was £1. 5s.0d whereas on a Hampshire estate, England, in 1844 the wage was 8s.6d. for the same amount The bricks from John's brickworks were selling at £4.0s.0d. per 1000, while from the Hampshire estate they cost £1.5s.0d. per 1000. The national weekly wage rates in England for 1850-51 were 10s.0d. for agricultural workers and 22s. 10d. for industrial workers. In the Staffordshire Potteries £2.0s. 0d. for a 72 hour working week was the maximum and 9.0d. the minimum wage.

As there is still no indication that Sarah is willing to join him John's patience seems to be at the limit, and he appears to be resigned to the possibility of never seeing her again, because from the tone of the letter he is more concerned about the acquisition of a pugmill. He has issued an ultimatum to her, but has softened it a little by offering to bring out her father and Joseph, John's youngest brother. He seems to be very concerned for Thomas's welfare so it is surprising that he did not include him in the package - perhaps he felt that he would not pass the stringent emigration conditions of entry.

Did Sarah use the excuse of not wanting to leave her father to justify her not joining him in South Australia?

After nearly five years away from home, he was still interested in

the progress of the different chapels, and he had received magazines giving details of 'the bretheren at Hednesford' and 'the
bretheren at Pogey Lane'. There was a Primitive Methodist Chapel
at Littleworth, Hednesford which was built in 1850, and it is
presumed this is the one referred to, and a small chapel with its own
cemetery, built in 1842 in Girton Road, Cannock, known in those
days as Podgy Lane. These sites were all at the extreme limits of the
village, and reflect the way in which evangelical Dissent was held
as disreputable and best confined to the margins of respectable
society.

Very soon after receiving this letter, Sarah must have taken a deep
breath and made the biggest decision of her life, for on 11th
December 1854, at the age of thirty-three years, she and four year
old Joseph John, arrived in South Australia on board the 'Marion'.
Perhaps John was on the quayside to meet her and the son he had
never seen, and it is noticeable in the letters to date that he never
mentioned him by name.

Had John changed in the years he had been in South Australia?
Had the upheaval had much impact on Sarah? If she had led a
sheltered life before, life on board ship would have opened her eyes
to a world she would not have known existed. The journey would
have been fraught with anxiety for her young son, and she would
have given priority to his protection and welfare. She may have
been very worried that her husband would not be pleased at the
length of time it had taken her to join him, and anxious that her son
would take a liking to the father he did not know. John would no
doubt be anxious to make them feel at home from the start, as it
would have been of benefit to him to have a wife to share his
burdens and help him achieve his goals.

But what had she let herself in for?

Mrs. Mary Burrows, who wrote the *History of Riverton,* describes

59

the life of farmers in the early days. "Eucalypts which fell to the axe became the slabs for the first huts, fuel for the first fires. Wattle and daub huts appeared in many places. The rafters were limbs from trees and the roofs were thatched like those they had left behind in the land of their birth, with reeds, or straw, or slabs sealed with clay. Make-shift materials finished off interiors of the first small homes. A ceiling was improvised from calico which flapped noisily on windy days. When the ceiling rippled and shook, the family knew that yet another snake was slithering above them. Calico was used instead of glass for windows too. All this calico came as flour bags which, after the flour was used, were ripped and sewn to serve a purpose. Caul fat from sheep was boiled down to make soap and candles. The little wives of the immigrants had fled their bonnet strings and faced inland to ease and share the labours of their husbands. The first lonely ones are still the symbol of high courage and endurance.Everyone on the farm helped build the cottages and

Bullocks used in clearing the land

each family made its own furniture. In the 'forties and 'fifties, the land was still in its virgin state. The settlers cleared a little more

60

land each year, thus gradually increasing their cropping area. A farmer who had forty acres in crop was a big farmer.... wheat was the cereal grown. Each settler kept a few cows. Weekly trips were made with the bullock wagons to carry dairy produce to Adelaide, Wallaroo, Kapunda or Burra. In slack times on the farm, settlers eked out their farm earnings by carrying provisions of coal for the miners of Burra or Kapunda, or wool for the pastoralists."

It would be fairly safe to assume that Sarah would not be greeted with quite such primitive conditions, as John would surely have built himself a house in brick, but other conditions would have been very typical.

It is some time before John writes again, but it is quite clear that there has been a change of address. Although in 1854 he had bought and sold 40 acres of land at a profit, and had thought about starting another brickworks, it seems that in the space of twelve months he had bought 160 acres of land at Head of the Light, Saddleworth, and called the farm Summer-hill Farm. Was it coincidence that where Sarah's father lived in England, there was a place very close at hand called Summer-hill, which was situated midway between Wednesbury and Tipton in Staffordshire. Later evidence reveals that although the address on the letter was Head of the Light, Saddleworth, the actual place was the township of Steelton, seven miles from Saddleworth.

December 25 1855 Head of the Light

Dear and honoured Parents,

This comes to you with our kindest love to you, hoping to find you all well as it leaves us at this time. Thank the Lord for all his

61

mercies; I must beg to be excused for delaying writing to you, it is not because ! had forgotten you, but I have not been disposed to write.I am now living upon the farm upon the Light River where I hope to remain as long as I am in the colony. I find that there is a great deal of labour to be done upon entering upon a open piece of land of 260 acres before there is much to come in. I have got my house builded and 80 acres fenced in, we fence in with post and rails in this country, which makes enclosed land valuable. I have not been able to cultivate any of my own land this season, but I have some ready for another if I should be spared to do it. I have some wheat and barley in a neighbours land and I am reaping it now; the weather is very warm here and the height of harvest with us, and I expect with you frost and snow and dead of winter. I hope to have as much wheat as will keep the house, and barley to feed my pigs; I have 3 sows in pig which I hope to feed after pigging.I have a nice lot of cattle which I hope will do well next season, we have had but few in milk this summer but I hope we shall have 20 or more in milk this coming season. We have a nice lot of cheese which we are going to take to Adelaide in a few days, after harvest is over which will realise about one shilling per pound.We have had a very trying time in this colony, there being a failure in the crops last harvest. Flour was very dear, it was sold at the copper mines as high as £8.0s.0d per bag. We have got an abundant harvest and flour is selling at £2.4s.0d per bag. Other things are pretty reasonable, we have sold our butter salt at 1s.8d per pound. I hope to make about £300 out of my dairy next year. Sarah has seen to the cheese and butter and managed it well. Joseph John is a fine useful boy, he can fetch in the cows and bullocks and knows them as well as I do, I intend to buy him a pony and then he will be as useful as a man to me. We keep a servant woman to milk and I have another *blessing befallen me, the Lord has given me another son and his name is Samuel Daniel, one of the finest children in the colony. He was born 21st September.*

I received a letter from Elizabeth a few weeks ago and one from Sarah's father, they want us to come back but I cannot think of returning until I have enough to keep me without a master. If could get a nice little farm somewhere near Cannock, or a public house I should not mind returning. If I had a place like Clefts would suit me; I do not know how he is doing, if he should like to sell his place I would like to buy it. Ask him if he would sell it and what he would like for it, and if he will send me word and the lowest he will take for it. My wife has got the home fever very bad, but I can do here very well. Joseph I think stood in his own light in not coming to me; he might in a few years done him some good but as he is wed he must do as well as he can.

Give my kind love to Aunt Tomlinson and my cousins, I suppose they are all grown men by this. I do not know how Thomas is doing but middling. My son Jo John send his kind love to you and Mother and Uncle Joseph. Sarah send her kind love to all, give my kind love to all enquiring friends and except the same yourself and we remain your loving son and daughter

John and Sarah Pickering

Back of letter: *Joseph sends that feather to Elizabeth his Aunt. He said one day his Grandfather would laugh to see him driving the bullocks with a whip about 14ft long*

Directions: John Pickering
Somer Hill Farm, Head of the Light
Near Saddleworth, South Australia
A kiss from the youngest Samuel Daniel

The most interesting point of this letter is the fact that just nine months after landing in South Australia, Sarah, on 21 September 1855, gave birth to another son Samuel Daniel. However, this does not seem to have alleviated her 'home fever', perhaps only made it worse; maybe longing for her father to see his second grandson. It speaks volumes for her character that despite having to get used to a strange country very quickly, and giving birth to a second child, she has been able to cope with life on the farm pretty well. Did she have any such training before joining John? Six year old Joseph John seems to have settled down and made himself useful, children, as usual, proving more adaptable than adults.

As an extract from A.P. Harvey's book *I Called it Salisbury* points out, "Regardless of the season, women, too, had plenty of work to do. Living off the land meant that they were compelled to exercise a variety of highly valuable occupations. In the house there was sewing, baking, candlemaking, carding and spinning, providing stores for winter, curing meat, preserving fruits, making jam and often home made wines such as blackberry and parsnip. Outside they had to tend to sheep, pigs, cows and poultry, and to look after the dairy. All these chores fell to the wives or female servants of the man on the land.

The work did not stop for the men, either, between tilling lime and harvest. Most settlers engaged in agriculture used those months for clearing the land of scrubwood and trees. The small timber was then carted to be made into posts and rails for fences, while the large limber was used in building projects."

A William Clift aged 55, together with his wife and family, appear in the 1851 Census for Cheslyn Hay, near Cannock, Staffordshire, with the occupation of farmer of 130 acres. Perhaps this was this the man John held in such high esteem.

Joseph, John's youngest brother, still living in the family home, married Harriet Parker on 25th June 1855 at the Parish Church at Church Eaton. Joseph was aged 25 years and Harriet 35 years of age.

Aunt Tomlinson was John's father's sister, Elizabeth, second wife of George Tomlinson, bricklayer, mentioned previously; his first wife being Jane, another sister. Jane had had three children, George, Jane and Georgiana. Within seven years, Jane and her three children had died, leaving George a widower with no family.

At that time in England it was illegal to marry your wife's sister, but George attempted to do just that on 27 January 1828 at St. Luke's Parish church, Cannock, the Banns being read for the second time. However, on the first reading of the Banns, a curate was standing in for the vicar, who had officiated at the first marriage. The vicar returned for the second reading, and the Banns were withdrawn and the note made, "parties within the prohibited degrees". Not to be put off, on 17 March 1828 at St. Peter's Collegiate Church, Wolverhampton, a marriage ceremony took place: a much bigger church, in a much larger town ten miles away, and presumably where no one knew them. Their haste and concern is perhaps understandable when we see that a son, George, was born on 11 May, 1828, followed by John, Thomas, James and Edwin - these five sons surviving into adulthood, but only until their middle thirties.

Extracts from Mrs. Bellman's *History of Steelton* portray the area in which the Pickering family lived and worked and became an integral part of the community.

"After the state of South Australia was settled in 1836 the land to the north of Adelaide was gradually opened up as the colonists sought to establish themselves on farms of their own. One of the chief factors in the development to the north was the discovery of copper at Kapunda in 1843 and at the Burra Burra in 1845. Small settlements sprang up along the copper route as stopping places for the bullock teams carting the copper ore and for the stage coaches which operated between Adelaide and the Burn.

The River Light which forms the valley in which Steelton is situated rises to the north of Waterloo, and was named after Colonel William Light, the well known surveyor of the city of Adelaide. The native name was "Yarra-linka". The Light received its title due to its length, not breadth, and many small creeks empty their water into the Light.

In the Steelton area the Light runs through a fertile valley and the district has a Mediterranean climate, the winters being wet and cold and the summers hot and dry. The winter rains usually come in the form of showers brought by the westerly winds while summer rain is often brought by thunderstorms. Rainfall over the years has averaged between 17 and 18 inches per year but has proved fairly reliable as a source of water with occasional drought years, when water has had to he carted for stock and household use, as the dams become dry and rainwater tanks are drained.

The land in its virgin state was covered in peppermint gum scrub with a sprinkling of blue gums, she-oaks and wattle trees. When the first settlers arrived they began to clear the land so that it could be used for agriculture.

By the end of 1855 there were quite a few families settled in Steelton, and it seems that the families of John Baillie, William Batts, William Blackaby, George Blake, James Brown, William Buchanan, Robert Hazell, Ebenezer Holder, Josiah Hunt, Henry Ivett, Jeremiah Jones, Joseph Kinsey, Martin McNamara, William and James Mahood, Joseph Bass Miller, John Pickering, William

Rawlins, Andrew Steele, John Tallack and Sampson Webb were among the first to settle in the township.

These pioneers travelled to Steelton in bullock drays bringing all their worldly possessions with them. The journey, usually from the districts to the north of Adelaide, took many days as they brought stock with them which had to be rested, fed and watered. On arrival at their destination they would have lived in tents until they erected their first rough houses which were made of stone and mud (pug), or wattle and daub, with thatched roofs with ceilings of flour bags. Firstly however, they would have had to make rough enclosures to keep their flock from straying. Most dwellings were near a creek or waterhole but as some of the smaller creeks dried up in the summer, the stock were taken to the River Light to water and small supplies carted home on the dray in wooden casks.

It must have been very frightening for the women especially, as there were so many aborigines living in the area. They used to walk up and down the Light and the surrounding scrubs holding their corroborees and having numerous fights. On the whole the aborigines did not cause any trouble and as they became used to the white people they would come to their houses and ask for flour, sugar and tea. This often made the women nervous if the men were not at home. On one occasion a young lubra rushed into the home of William and Mary Rawlins and hid under the sofa for protection. She had run away from her tribe and joined another tribe and they were looking for her. They did not find the house as it was hidden by thick scrub. She left late in the evening, after a good meals and taking some food with her she set off to find her way back to her own tribe. Had the other tribe caught her she would have been killed.

There were also wild dogs in the area which were a problem when sheep were introduced to the district, and they had to be minded at night to keep them safe. The men and children herded sheep until fences were built, sheep proof soft wire was £8.0s.0d. a ton. Post and rail fences were made with split logs and a three wired fence was used with branches of trees and brush piled up along the bottom to make them sheep proof.

The cattle that the settlers brought with them provided meat, milk and butter. The meat was salted down to preserve it and it was kept in wooden casks. Possibly the men shot kangaroos for meat, and as the lads used to enjoy possuming perhaps they also had a possum stew, for variety. The women made their own bread, soap and candles, Burra and Kapunda were the nearest large towns and the produce was carted there on bullock drays. The passing bullockies acted as messenger boys carting goods to and from the mining towns for the farmers. Supplies of flour, sugar, salt, tea and farm commodities were bought from these towns. The settlements of Marrabel to the south and Waterloo to the north gradually developed into small towns and Saddleworth, miles to the west, grew from a few houses into a much larger centre.

In the first years of settlement most of the 80 acre sections had houses on them but the migrants found that the soil was not rich enough to support a family on so small a farm, and gradually they moved out to other areas, selling their blocks to neighbouring farmers. Many of these rented their houses and made a living by working casually for the larger land owners.

The farmers grew grain and horses were their source of power. They kept cows for milk and butter, cattle and sheep for meat and pigs for the winter meat, as well as geese and poultry to supplement their diet. They were pretty well self-sufficient with their candlestick makers, soap making, coffee grinders and sausage making machines. They made their own bread and cake in their enclosed woodburning stone stoves.

Vegetable gardens were cultivated where possible and were mostly situated near a dam or well for convenience of watering. Wells and dams were made as soon as the settlers could make time to do so as it was vital to conserve as much water as possible.

Sept 15th 1856 Sumer Hill Head of the Light

Dear Mother and Father,

I write to you again in answer to a letter received from you bearing date May 6th hoping this will find you quite well and happy as it leaves us at this time. Thank God for all his mercies. I was glad to hear from you for I thought it was a long time since I heard from you, and I suppose you thought the same by concluding that I was dead, but I will endeavour to write a little oftener I have been so busy with the things of this world that my time has been so occupied; I hope to be less engaged after a short time. I have had a deal to do as you may think, entering upon 160 acres of naked land, but by the blessing of God I have made something to be seen since I entered upon it. Our fencing in this country consists of posts and rails, I have enclosed one 80 acres in dividing it into 2 fields, the one on which my house is upon is about 36 acres, the other is a corn and gardening about 44 acres. I have a nice piece of wheat and barley sown this year which will be as much as I think I shall consume, and! have a good piece broken up for fallow. You must understand we cannot plough like you can there. The land requires ploughing in the winter while wet, the summer the land is powder dry. when the rains begin that is about the end of April then the sowing commences, which generally performed as quick as possible

69

on account of it being ready before the ojfwinds come, which dry up the ground and the corn harvest generally begins at the end of November, and by Christmas is in. This season there has been an insect upon the cabbage and destroyed them, and also the turnips; in many places they say it is upon the wheat. In many places the vegetables have been very scarce. I have sold many of those white stone turnips at 10d and 1s. 0d per dozen. Sarah keeps a servant and they are making about 6 cheeses per week some of them about 50 pounds each. Cheese is about 1s 0d per pound, butter 1s. 6d per pound.

I have had 12 cows calved and there are 14 more to calve this year. I rear all the calves and I buy all the cattle that I can, I have a run on the Crown Land for which to run them upon, by paying 6d per head per year. Seven sows in pig 2 fat in the sty, 6 store ones ready to fatten when the barley is ripe. By the end of this month I shall have the other 80 acres of land enclosed, as you may think it has been a busy time at our house. I have bought Joseph John a pony and a new saddle, who is become a fine son. He is learning to ride and will soon be able to ride in the cows; and that will save me 5s. 0d per week and keep, which I have to pay a boy. He is I think one of the cleverest boys in the colony he is like a man for (?). Samuel Daniel is a fine child, it would do you good to see him, he is as big a boy as ever saw of his size (sic). He is not twelve months old and he can go about the house by himself. You did not say whether Joseph's wife had any child; I am glad to hear that he is doing well and comfortable; poor Tom, he will always be in the mire of poverty I am afraid, how easy to do bad.

My wife, she is continuously talking of home, but I should like to end my days in my mother land, yet I should not like to return without having enough to live upon. I think I could, with a little business such as Clifts place, if 1 could buy it would suit me, but I would not like to rent again. I have been from you 10 years I think with the blessings of God to be able to return. I suppose that with my stock farm, and brickyard is worth £1200 or more money and if I could return to England with £2000 clear I would come. I am astonished when I look round me and see what I have done in so short a time, landing in this colony with 1/8d in my pocket; it is the Lord's doings and it is marvellous in our eyes.

Haycarting early 1900

Wheat harvesting before tractors

And now dear parents, I commend you to God and the word of his grace, which is able to make you wise into Salvation through faith that is in him. Give my kind love to my poor Aunt Tomlinson, I hope her sons are good to her, my love to Jo and wife, Clift and children, my sister (?) and receive the same from your son and daughter

JSP

This letter speaks for itself in as much as the family seem very settled, making money and rapid progress A small sign of prosperity was the acquisition of a pony for Joseph John. According to H. John Lewis's book *Salisbury, A History of Town and District;* "Bullocks were cheap in comparison with horses and they were used extensively from the first days of settlement. In the absence of roads they were very dependable and adapted themselves to rough conditions. They went as straight as possible, uphill and down dale, to their destination and did not require a graded track. That they were slow is demonstrated by the fact that they made only one trip a day between Gleneig and Adelaide.

"By 1839 there were 200 horses in South Australia, but they were too costly except for wealthy people. It is said that Governor Gawler paid £136 for a horse whereas bullocks could be purchased for £36 a head."

John was however saving money on wages to pay a boy, proving what an astute business man he was. At this time, Joseph, now a married man, was living in the family home, with his father, and as yet with no children, and news of Aunt Tomlinson seems to have given cause for concern. She was by this time a widow, her husband George having died in 1852, and by November 1861 she had died, leaving five sons, all of whom had passed away by 1871.

It appears that John retained ownership of the brickyard although he was now living about 70 miles away in the bush, and it is possible that Joseph Bass Miller continued to run that side of the business.

The religious expressions used in the letter were typical of those used by Primitive Methodists and were constantly on their lips. Joseph Ritson, in *The Romance of Primitive Methodism,* says, "Into the story of the Primitive Methodist Church there enters to an unusual degree the element of the wonderful and even the mysterious. From the early days the men and women who had been associated with it were filled with astonishment as they contemplated the humility of its origins, the lowliness of its agents and the marvellous manner in which it had grown.

Mrs Bellman's *History of Steelton District* gives further insights into the life of the settlers: "The wheat was carted by bullock wagons until horses became more readily available. As the farmers cleared their land they began to cultivate their few acres to grow wheat. The scrub was cleared with axes and bullock or horse drawn tree pullers. Horses were expensive as shown by items in Sampson Webb's account book when on 5th December, 1861, he purchased one black mare for £20.0s.0d. Single furrow ploughs drawn by horses were used in the early days. These ploughs were imported from England, but with the growth of the colony much employment was provided for wheelwrights, blacksmiths and saddlers who settled in most localities and made implements for farmers. In the early days grain was broadcast by hand."

The days of farming with horses were hard, long days when the farmer rose about 5 o'clock, or earlier in the busy times, to feed the horses which were kept in the stables overnight from mid April till early September. They cleaned out the stables, had breakfast, harnessed up the horses about 7.30a.m. and set out for the paddock, which might be more than a mile away. The midday meal was eaten by a dam where the horse teams were watered and fed with their nose bags. At about 4.30 p.m. a start was made for home, the horses walking briskly in eagerness to get home. The farmer after walking behind the harrows or single furrow plough all day did not need any sleeping pills at night.

In the small township of Steelton there were now a school, Primitive Methodist Chapel, Post Office Store, Hotel, at least two blacksmiths, a bootmaker, a butcher and a store and wine shop run by the Pickering family. John and Sarah Ann Pickering were among the early settlers who attended the Pancharpoo Chapel and Sunday School, although they lived to the north on section 1001 where Kunden School is now situated. The school hill in those days was known as "Pickering's Pinch". The Kinsey family also owned a little shop in Steelton.

Pancharpoo Primitive Methodist Church was built at Steelton in

Pancharpoo Primitive Methodist church built at Steelton in 1858. The last regular service was held in 1964. Photograph taken 1907

74

1858 on land owned by Mr. Joseph Kinsey. The original name was
"Reoboth", which is a Hebrew word meaning "The Lord hath made
room", the name Pancharpoo is a native word, which could mean
"on the watch for kangaroos", suggesting that the aborigines lay in
wait as kangaroos returned from their drink at the River Light.

Before the building of Pancharpoo Chapel, meetings were held at
Mr and Mrs Josiah Hunt's cottage for about two years. Primitive
Methodist ministers on their way, on horseback, between Kapunda
and Burra, often found a haven of rest for themselves and fodder for
their horses. Mr Hunt presented the 'cause' with two tall brass
candle sticks. Now the said Rev. J. G. Wright was a very bright,
lively preacher. While demonstrating some thrilling point in his
address, with a flourish of his arms, Mr. Wright sent the brass
candle sticks flying and so the bewildered congregation were left in
the dark. The preacher went on without a pause saying, "Never
mind, my dear people, worse things happen at sea." Did he ever
realise how prophetic those last few words would apply to the
Pickering family?

The Rev. J.G. Wright wrote the following account of the opening
of the chapel for the old Primitive Methodist Record *Light:*

"By the help of God on the 1st August, we opened our chapel at
this place; we have named it 'Reoboth'. For two years we had been
worshipping God in a small cottage, which was inconvenient, and
far too small to contain our congregation. But the Lord hath made
us a room by disposing the hearts of the settlers to erect a suitable
place of worship. It is a neat stone building, after the Gothic style.
Mr. H.B. Thomas preached in the morning and afternoon, and the
writer at night. As usual on such occasions, on the following day, a
delightful tea meeting was held, provided gratuitously by a few of
the warm hearted ladies, who had the pleasure to see a large and

respectable gathering of their friends. Tea being over, the assembly were addressed by Messrs. Thomas, Rowe and Dale; whose speeches were interesting and full of life. The amount raised by contributions was £60. 14s.2d. The Trustees tendered their thanks to Messrs. Webb, Dale, Rallet, Miller, Buchanan, Mrs. Pickering and her two children, and others for their liberal donations in money, and to Messrs. Hallet, Brown, Pickering, Bailey, Olley and Webb for labouring, amounting to £121 .0.0d. As a school is much needed in the neighbourhood, the Trustees intend the chapel to be used as a school-house, and may it be made a great blessing to the people." The cost of the building was £231.2s.4d. and the first trustees were J. G. Wright (minister), who came from Kapunda, Samuel Olley, S. Miller, Sampson Webb and John Pickering. The building was used as a school for about six years during which time Mr. Joseph Kinsey was the teacher.

The Pancharpoo Chapel was the focal point for the Methodists at Steelton and Sunday was the day of the week when they worshipped but also met each other socially and tea meetings were held on week nights and later a mid-week service on Wednesday nights. Pancharpoo became the head of the Circuit consisting of the following thirteen churches: Pancharpoo, Riverton, Saddleworth, Mintaro, Kollyowha (Tothill's Creek), Coghill's Creek, Waterloo, Glendore (Black Springs), Burton (Manoora), Auburn, Twyford (Tothill's Belt), Emu Flats and Emu Belt.

John Pickering's Chapel Account Book Trustee 1858 records:

8.12.62   Miss Pickering Donation £1.0.0d.
6. 4.63   Mrs Pickering Donation £2.0.0d
27.12.63   Mrs. Pickering Donation £3.0.0d Mr. Joseph Pickering
           Donation £1. 0.0d.

In 1860 the Pancharpoo congregation decided to build a house for their minister and the costs listed in the account book for the building came to a modest £22. 9. 1d.

1858 Source of the River
Light, Somerhill

My Dear Father and Mother, Brothers and Sister,
After many a time talking about you and home, I again write to you hoping to find you all in good health as it leaves us at this time; thank God for ever
We received a letter from Sister Elizabeth last night, which was gladly received, and a newspaper, and as the scriptures says, 'water to a thirsty man is sweet' so is news from a far country, although the paper upon which it was wrote was bad and the writing worse still; it is with much difficulty we do make it out
We are still living up the country, about 75 miles from Adelaide and 25 from the Burra Burra mines, which is our market for our produce. I hope to be able to go there every week; after a few weeks our cows will be calving down now rapidly so the butter, cheese, eggs, pork, turnips, potato and other things. We shall have a deal of one sort or another to part with, we have 25 cows that will calve this season, we have 3 sows that have pigs this week and 4 more in pig beside store ones. We have about 50 head of poultry, 4 geese, 2 ganders, 25 acres of corn in 2 teams of bullocks and drays. We have 2 horses and I bought a beautiful spring cart to go to market with. We have a beautiful stock of young cattle, and I have but returned home but a few days from Adelaide where I had been, and laid out more than £200 in goods to begin a shop.

77

There is no shops within miles of us, and Sarah said she could manage it We keep a man and women servants, and I expect we shall want another this season if Sarah does much business in the store. My children are 2 fine healthy boys. Joseph John is as yourself as a man in many things with pigs and cattle. He drove the bullocks to put the crop in this season and part of last season, he used to milk 2 cows night and morning, so that all that can work must about me. Samuel Daniel is a fine big boy runs about into all kinds of mischief and dirt I have given you a sketch of our position, so you may form some idea of what your poor wandering child has been doing since he left his father's house, and wandered into a far country in a distant land. My wife and me often talk of home and we should like to end our days at home. We often talk about returning, we still love our parents and it would afford us great joy in seeing and enjoying their company again, but I must see my way clear before we can return. I am but just got into a position to make money and I should not like to return to have to work for a master after being my own so long. I think that about £2000 laid out at interest would keep us comfortable in England so that I should have something for my children. I cannot tell whether we shall have any more or not, there is no sign at present, time alone will decide that matter when I look round and consider what has been accomplished in a short time by steady careful persevering industry, and blessings of my God upon my lab ours, I can say what hath God wrought by me, seeing I landed in this colony with 1s. 8d in my pocket in 1850.

I should like to form acquaintance with some honest shoemaker in England one that would get up good work; I could sell as many as 20 men could make, if they was good serviceable boots, and a great quantity of small ones. There comes a great many of boots and shoes

out into this country, but they are made so bad that they are not
worth buying. Shoemakers are charging £1.4. 0d. for men's working
boots, no better than is sold in Bilston market for 7s. 0d to 8s.0d..
Snobs are doing well in this country. When you write, send particu-
lars how Thomas is going on and Joseph, what... (?)... and where
living, how Clifts are doing and Aunt Tomlinson and her family
with Withnalls family, the good cause of Christ in the neighbour-
hood and how you are getting on for heaven, remember it is
journey and there must be a preparation for it - without holiness no
man shall see the Lord. Give my love to all and except the kindest
from your loving son, daughter

J.S.Pickering

This letter was not clearly dated, but it is estimated to have been
written around June 1857, as Sarah Jane was born on 26th April,
1858 and there is no mention of the pregnancy in this letter.

Although John seemed well established, the records show that he
did not purchase until December 1857, 80 acres, Section 1001 from
Robert Davenport, at a cost of £108 (Land Record Memorial
135/142), and a further 80 acres in August 1858 Section 1002 from
Roben Stuckey, Peter Dowding Prankherd for £185 (LRM
136/142). Presumably to help raise the money for this land, he sold,
in December 1857, Plots 75/76, the Brickworks site, to Samuel
Edwards for £30 (LRM 11/139), and Plot 53 for £10 (LRM 12/139);
again at a profit. Samuel Edwards is recorded in A.F. Harvey's *I
Called It Salisbury* as being the man who opened the first brick and
tile business in Salisbury. This record can now be 'set straight'.

John in the same month, mortgaged 60 acres of the land just purchased, 1001/1002, to Frederick White (LRM 224/142) for the sum of £400.

Steelton District History records: Land tides in South Australia had fallen into such chaos from speculation and private dealing in land during the 20 years since colonization that a new system was needed. In 1858 the Torrens land title system was devised by Robert Richard Torrens and this was passed into law by the State Government in spite of determined opposition. The Torrens Titles from 1858 onwards showed changes of ownership for all sections of land surveyed. Landowners were issued with titles but these were often dated 1858 or 1859 whereas the farmer had purchased and had occupied the land for some time prior to this date.

The reference to shoemakers in his letter is interesting, as both his father and grandfather were cordwainers (shoemakers), commonly known as 'snobs'. In England until the beginning of the twentieth century, every town and village had its shoemaker or cobbler. A cobbler repaired shoes, instead of making them. True shoemakers or 'snobs' considered themselves a little above mere cobblers and did not like being called by that name; they were also known as cordwainers. A shoe covered the foot, whereas a boot covered the foot, ankles and possibly more. 'Snob' was originally a Suffolk dialect word for a shoemaker or cobbler. It did not develop its modern meaning until the nineteenth century, when used by Thackeray to denote a social climber.

Shoemakers had a reputation for radical politics, hard drinking, a fondness for pets, especially songbirds, and ideas above their station. Many shoemakers were free thinkers and Dissenters, so details of them may be found in the archives of Nonconformist churches. This could well be where John inherited his radical views.

Thomas, the brother he was so concerned about in his letters home had been an apprentice shoemaker in Cannock, so the question must be asked - why did John refrain from sending for him, to rescue him from his life of what he believed to be poverty

John's mother's maiden name was Hannah Withnall, so the mention of the Withnall family would include all aunts, uncles and cousins on his mother's side of the family.

The whole tone of this letter conveys the message of a man taking everything is his stride, and daily gaining confidence in his own ability, but still with a longing for his homeland.

For the next three years there is a lapse in correspondence from John, which causes a great deal of concern, as during this time any one of a number of situations could have occurred. As mail was the only means of communication, the absence of letters home would create the impression of crisis and the family could only guess at the state of their well being or otherwise. Sarah's father, Joseph Sanders, became increasingly worried for their safety, and in August 1858 wrote to John Pickerill in Cannock.

August 11th 1858

My Dear Friends,

I write these few lines to you hoping they will find you all in good health as it leaves me, very uncomfortable in mind about John and Sarah, for I have not heard from them almost twelve months since, and I am afraid there is something the matter with them. The last letter as I had from them was in October last and they promised to write to me in a few months, and I have never a one yet. That has been almost twelve months since. And will you please to write by the return of post to let me know whether you have heard from them

81

for I am uneasy in my mind about them.

Danial and Hannah Marsh sends their kind love to you and Elizabeth. Please to send me word when you come to Walsall and I will meet you there at the Three Tuns. My dear friends, God bless you all amen.

Please to direct for me to be left at Danial Marsh for me Joseph Sanders at Ocker Hill Tipton Staffordshire.

Amen God bless you all.

We know that Joseph Sanders was Sarah's father. As this letter was discovered with the rest of the letters, it is presumed that this letter was written by Sarah's father, to John's father in Cannock. It would seem that Joseph thought John's father might have had more recent news and vividly illustrates how anxious relatives in England were about their loved ones overseas. It is probable that Hannah was Sarah's sister, and Joseph's other daughter.

In the census of 1851, mention is made in the entry for the District of Tipton, at 76 Bilston Road, Ocker Hill, Daniel Marsh, aged 30, stocktaker, Hannah Marsh, aged 31 and Samuel Marsh aged 5. Daniel had been born in Sedgely, Hannah and Samuel at Tipton.

The Three Tuns was a public house in Walsall, and was possibly the venue suggested for their meeting, and would be about midway between Cannock and Tipton, and a distance of about ten miles for each to travel.

Apparently having had no reply from John's father to his previous letter, Joseph again wrote to Cannock on 7th September asking for information, but this time mentions, "I would have come over but I have got bad legs, would not walk that far."

Two years later, in February 1860, he still had not heard from

John and Sarah and was frantic with worry. It also appears that he was now living with the Marsh family at Tipton.

However, two months later John's father in Cannock received the following letter:

April 30 1860   River Light, Tothill Creek

Dear Father, Mother, Brother, Sister,

I send these few lines to you hoping they will find you all well as it leaves us at present, with the exception of Sarah. It has been a long time since I wrote to you so that there has been many changes since then at home and abroad. I have battled with the world for now ten years in this colony, and I thought of returning by this time, but I find I'm not prepared yet. I think should the Lord spare and continue to prosper me for two years more, I shall be able to be without a master if I return to England. We have a great deal under hand at this time, but I am getting my business into less space. I have given up agriculture farm, and turned my attention to sheep farming. I find it to be much profitable. We have bought about 1800 acres of land and keep two shepherds; we lambed down last season 750 lambs and we have now 1500 ewes to lamb this season. The lambing season is just commenced, we have about 20 dropped and in a month from this time to have 500 in, and in a six weeks to have 1000 more lambs. We made £377 of our wool last season and about £400 of our lambs; this year we have half as many more. I think there will be a reaction in trade, the colony is in a very bad state at present, money is scarce and the prices of things very high. I will send you a newspaper and you will see the price of things.

The Goldfields lately found out is stripping this colony with men it is all the talk of to the diggings, I believe in two months time there will not be 20 men on the Light where I live, for 10 miles; but will be gone so that labour will be very scarce and dear. I think land will be very dear when men return from the diggings, then I shall sell out and come back to you again. I think I shall be able to leave £1000 in the colony at 10% which will bring me in £100 a year and £1000 with me; I shall be able, with carefulness, to live without a master

I have sold the farm I lived upon for £500, to be paid £200 in 2 years and £300 in 4 years bearing interest at £40 a year, and I have builded me a large new house with eight rooms on the ground in which we are living in, and keeping a general store and butchering. But I built it for a public house and I believe I shall sell it for one as soon as the diggers come back with the gold. I expect to get £1500 for it. Me and my wife are tired of business and cannot stand so much hard work as we have our farm, family, is heavy and wants more. Joseph John is a fine boy he can ride a horse anywhere or drive a team of bullocks. Sam Daniel is a big nugget, Sarah Ann is turned two years out, and George Wright is our youngest, he was baptized a fortnight ago but Sarah is not so well after her confinement, and not likely to be so stout as formerly.

I should like for you to send me as much information about things as you can, how you are doing, how your health is, what your prospects are, the position of the whole family, the state of the kin folks and etc. Give my kind love to all family connections and en quiring friends, and remaining your affectionate son and daughter

John Sarah Pickering April 31 (sic) 1860.

Address Mr J. Pickering Store Keeper River Light Tothill Creek, South Australia

A gap of almost three years and what a change, no wonder John did not have time to write home. It has not as yet been proved in the records that this land was purchased, but there is no reason to doubt it. Although he has said he has built a 'large new house' it will be noted at the time of writing, his address was still River Light Tothill Creek.

Sarah Jane was born 26 April, 1858 and George Wright in April 1860. Was George Wright, the youngest child, named after John Gibbon Wright's son George? Sadly he had died by September 1862 although no exact dates are known. However, according to his grave stone he was 13 months old when he passed away. This headstone was discovered and unearthed from the floor of the stable where the present owner of Summerhill Farm, now renamed Talla Walla, lives. Mr. Ervyn Behn, a friend of Mrs. Bellman the Steelton historian asked her if it was of any interest to her! She of course, already having made contact with me, wrote to me post haste.

Why was it there? As there was no cemetery at Pancharpoo Chapel at the time of his death, the next best thing would be to be buried at home. This headstone has survived in remarkably good condition.

The farm he sold for £500 could well be the one that was lived in during 1855, and was put to arable farming. During February 1861 John was again busy acquiring land but this time leasing and not buying it. The reason for this is not clear, but it could be that this time he was looking to make the profit from the business rather than speculating on the buying and selling of land. His partner in this venture was Angus Cameron, of whom very little is known at this stage, but together they took on a 14 year lease of 405 acres, Sections 2113/5/6/7/2112 near Port Wakefield, from George Strickland Kingston, for a rent of £50.0.0d. per annum. Both were stated as sheep farmers, in the Counties of Gawler and Stanley. Another 160 acres, Sections 2118/9 was leased for 14 years from John Battey Thorngate (England) at a rent of £20 per annum.

The land which he had mortgaged to Frederick White for £400 in August 1858 he regained for £400 on 7 March 1861. On 1 May, 1861 602 acres, Section 177 was transferred from John Pickering and Angus Cameron to William Martin and a sum of money of £750 to or from Edward William Wright, and £100 to or from John Pickering and Angus Cameron was involved. At this stage no more information is to hand and this transaction is not properly understood.

In June 1861, in the County of Light, Section 1001 plus Public House, was leased from John Pickering to Charles Gladlow, for a period of five years, at a cost of £75 for the first year, and £100 per annum after, with the right to purchase during the lease 'The Light Hotel' for the sum of £1250.

In July, 1862, shortly before he writes his last letter, between Adelaide and Port Wakefield, John Pickering and Angus Cameron took up a lease for one year of 35 square miles at a cost of £42.0.0d. per annum, although the entry was not made in the land register until 5 November 1862.

From the date of the previous letter, John had been extremely busy with his business transactions, consolidating, reorganising and extending, all at the same time.

The next letter is written to Daniel and Hannah Marsh, who presumably had been the ones responsible for imparting the sad news of the death of Sarah's father, Joseph Sanders. This lends weight to the theory that Hannah was Sarah's sister.

It is obvious that John has not received a letter from his father in Cannock for a long time, and as this letter was tied together with the rest, it stirs the imagination that when Daniel and Hannah had read it they either posted it on to Cannock, or went to pay a visit, and decided that John's father could keep it.

Port Wakefield Sep 14 1862

My Dear Brother and Sister,

We received your letter containing the information of our Father's death, but it affords us pleasure to hear that his end was peace. Knowing that we must all die and come to the house appointed for all living. We certainly felt it to be a great shock on us, filling this house with sorrow; my dear wife was quite ill and went to bed. Joseph John cried until his eyes was red; Samuel Daniel said Grandfather was dead, Sarah Jane said she had only one Grandfather now. Our youngest son, George Wright is gone to the better land, so we have only three children. Joseph John is useful as a man, Samuel Daniel is a nice quiet boy, but Sarah Jane is as sharp as a needle. My dear wife does not enjoy her health as we would wish; I am thankful I have tolerable share of health, which is necessary in this country, customs and manners being very different here. Should providence smile on my efforts, a year or two more I will try to see our native land again, for I am getting tired of this colony. I have toiled hard since I let you and begin to want to take it easy; human nature wants rest.

87

We are living at Port Wakefield, on a sheep run, having let the farm on the Light for £30.0.0d. per annum, with the public house we have let for £100.0.0d a year rent and have as much as we can do with the sheep. We have 3000 sheep and shearing will commence with us on the 20th of this month, which will take a month or more to shear them; it will be a busy time for us for a few weeks. Sarah keeps a store and there is a good deal of wool shipped to England at this port. The only business done is the wool, which takes about three months, and after that you will be weeks and not see anyone but your own people. We have not place of worship nearer that 20 miles, so that to get to Adelaide or any town is a treat to spend the Sunday.

Mrs and me went over to Wallaroo on a Saturday, 40 miles, to the chapel opening. Wallaroo is the new copper mines which bids fair to eclipse the world for copper, the far found Burra Burra being only a speck to it. Mrs was over at Mrs Hills, that is Mr Parkins (?Parkers) Daughter and was quite at home, it is the only place that we find anything like England, it is like being at Portobello or Bloomfield or Tipton. We often talk over these places when we get together. Sarah was there when she received the letter from her father and he said he had been seeing you and that you had got the things all safe.

Dear Brother and Sister, I should be glad if you would send me any information about Cannock, as I have not heard any particulars about my mother-in-law, whether she is dead or alive and (?) Is living with my Father, as you mentioned in your letter that Joseph was living with Father, and where Elizabeth is and Tom, and what they are doing at Norton, as I have not heard any particulars about them. I suppose my Father is a little old man by this time and not able to do anything, but I shall write to him after shearing is over and have more time. If all things go right we shall be in Adelaide about Christmas, and will send you the likeness of the children. The vessel that brought your things will be in about that time and we will send by Captain Angel to you. Mr. and Mrs. Hill send their love to you and would like to see your face, she thinks you are something like Staffordshire.

Dear Brother, I wish you would make enquiry at some of the foundries what they would cast me a pump complete. To draw water out of a well 80 feet deep to work by horse power, and send word in the next letter all the particulars. I think I could get them much cheaper there than here, there are a good many sent out from your part but the Agents get so much on them which makes them come very dear. The pipes of the pump to be a four inch bore.

We conclude with our kindest love to you my dear Brother and Sister, and Samuel my nephew; I suppose you are a big man by this time. Remain yours truly,

John and Sarah Pickering
To Daniel and Hannah Marsh
Hockerhill England

Back of letter:-
My dear Sister, I will send you another letter soon my self

It would seem that John has also leased the farm on The Light at a rent of £30.0.0d. per annum. There is no record as yet of the death of George Wright.

"If all things go right, we shall be in Adelaide about Christmas".
Even as this letter was travelling on its way to England, John
Pickering's story had ended.

We can only imagine how the news was imparted to John's family
back in the old country, but it is obvious that Hannah. was still in
touch with both sides as the following letter illustrates:-

Strathalbyn
South Australia May 24/64

My Dear Grandfather,

*No doubt you have thought it strange that we have not written you
so long. Not having heard from you so long a time, we did not know
whether you were living or not.*

*Mother wrote to Aunt Hannah to ask her about you, we had a
letter by the last mail, saying you were still alive, of course you
have heard of my Father's death. We sold the sheep and went back
to our old place to live.*

*Mother has married again (after Christmas) to John Tallack, a
Primitive Methodist Minister; he is stationed at Strathalbyn where
we now live, he is very kind to us and we like him very much.
Samuel is getting a fine lad, we go to school together.*

*Sarah Jane is got a big girl and full of spirit. We are very
comfortable. I hope to remain at school for two years longer. We
are now living in a very nice town which will afford us many
advantages. We have before always lived in the bush. I hope you*

90

are well, you must be getting a very old man. I hope you have a good prospect for another world and that God will give you grace unto the end.

The family all join in kind love to you. We shall be glad to hear from you, being my first attempt you will please excuse my short letter,

Accept the kind love of
Your affectionate Nephew ('Nephew' crossed out and replaced with 'Grandson'

Joseph John Pickering

This was the last letter in the collection - the end of the story. Or only the beginning?

Chapter 4

It was decided to set about trying to find the cause of this untimely death - was it through illness, or some tragic accident on the farm?

Very early on in the research, information received from the South Australian Genealogy and Heraldry Society (SAGHS) revealed:

The Adelaide Register, 27 October 1862:

15th October 1862, drowned by the capsizing of the cutter 'Sarah' on voyage from Port Wakefield to Port Adelaide, John PICKER-ING, Sheepfarmer, of Port Wakefield, late of Staffordshire, England.

The researcher also made the following comments:

"Another sheepfarmer, Angus Cameron, was also drowned in the same incident. I don't know why they were sailing from Port Wakefield to Adelaide, as it is only a distance of about 60 miles, and would surely have been quicker by road."

What a piece of information to set an already curious mind on its relentless travels!

As the boat was named 'Sarah' and knowing the kind of man John was, I wondered if he had purchased a boat and named it after his own wife. As some of his land now bordered the coast, was he doing a survey from the sea to assess his assets?

Much later on, when limited research had started to piece the story together, a decision was made to hire a professional researcher to carry out on-the-spot research, and Andrew Peake did an admirable job. In addition he contacted the Australasian Maritime Historical Society, who could not be specific, offered various suggestions, adding that "at no time in that period was a vessel of that name enrolled in South Australia ... and the best you could hope for would be some passing reference in either the police or marine board file."

Not content with this reply, it was suggested that as the accident had been reported in *The Register,* a fuller account might be included in a later edition?

The reply was all that could have been hoped for, and included this report from Saturday 18 October 1862.

FATAL ACCIDENT IN THE GULF

Coroner's Inquest:

The steamer 'Sturt' which sailed on Thursday morning for Clinton, brought up in tow on her return early on Friday morning the cutter 'Sarah', which Captain Luxon reported to have picked up on the Gulf. Also the bodies of two men -William McKay, the master of the cutter, and Peter Johnson, a seaman - which were found drowned on board. The bodies were conveyed to an old store at the rear of the Britannia Hotel, and on Friday afternoon Dr. Woolforde held an inquest at the above house, when the following evidence was taken:

George McKay, sailmaker, deposed that he had identified one of the bodies as that of his son, William Mc Kay, and the other as that of Peter, a man in his son's employ. His son was 27 years of age and owned and sailed the cutter 'Sarah' which left the Port on Saturday for Pt. Wakefield. A young man named Henry Nell, and the deceased Peter, were also on board when the cutter sailed. The cutter was laden with a general cargo of stores. Witness's son had been accustomed to the sea for nearly twenty years.

Thomas Carr, water police constable, identified one of the bodies
as that of a man named Johnson, a foreigner, who belonged to the
cutter 'Sarah', but formerly lodged in the same house as the witness.

William Luxon, master of the steamer 'Sturt' stated that he left the
Port on Thursday morning at 8 o'clock for Clinton, and about 10
o'clock saw what appeared to be a vessel capsized about 7 miles
from Port Gawler. He steamed towards it and found it to be the
cutter 'Sarah', about two feet of her stern only being visible and
occasionally the masthead. He immediately made fast to it and
attempted to raise it, when the body of Johnson was seen on the
deck and taken on board the steamer. Finding that he could not
succeed in getting the cutter sufficiently out of the water to bale her
out, towed her on the flats where she was got upright and baled out
and the body of Mc Kay was found on the ballast in the hold was
removed to the steamer. He then left two men in charge of the cutter
and proceeded to Clinton, but called and took the cutter in tow on
returning to the Port. The day before was very squally and when he
found the cutter the sea was breaking on her. He could see nothing
to indicate carelessness but he believed she had been capsized in a
squall as the mainsail was torn; the main sheet was unrove and the
boom adrift. The jib-sheet was also loose.

John Schmidt, seaman, stated that he and another man owned the
cutter 'Maria', which left the Port on Saturday, in company with the
'Sarah'. On Wednesday morning the 'Maria' left Well's Creek, near
Port Arthur, and about 10 o'clock a breeze sprang up and they soon
afterwards saw the 'Sarah' ahead. Was gaining on the 'Sarah' when
he observed the hands on board set the gaff topsail. About 2 o'clock
a squall came on and witness lowered sail, but the 'Sarah' continued
with all sails set. Another squall came on between 2 and 4 o'clock
but all this time the 'Sarah' was considerably ahead. Witness
lowered the

sails and the squall was so violent that they could not see the length of the vessel in consequence of the spray. The dinghy belonging to the 'Maria' was carried away during the squall and when it moderated they hove to to pick it up - but nothing was then to be seen of the 'Sarah'. Could only see two men on board of the 'Sarah'. Witness could see the squalls coming before they struck the vessel.

The Coroner said he had no further evidence to offer but there appeared to be no doubt that the deceased men were accidentally drowned by the upsetting of the cutter during a squall. The jury overwhelmingly returned a verdict to that effect.

Captain Luxon stated that on board the cutter were found a parcel containing clothing to a female; also a portmanteau containing the uniform and apparel and some letters of a police trooper named Fox - but there was nothing to show that there were any other persons than those found on board the cutter at the time she capsized although there is every reason to believe that the young man Nell was returning in the cutter.

The deceased William McKay was a single man, and was very much respected in Port Adelaide.

No mention of John Pickering or Angus Cameron!

The Observer - Saturday 25 October 1862
THE RECENT ACCIDENT IN THE GULF - From information received from Port Wakefield it has been ascertained beyond doubt that when the cutter 'Sarah' (which was capsized in the Gulf during the gale of Wednesday week) left Port Wakefield there were on board at least five other persons besides those whose bodies were found with the vessel. Of this number were Messrs. Cameron and Pickering (squatters in the Port Wakefield district) and Henry Nell, who left Port Wakefield with the cutter for the trip. Fuller partic-

ulars will be found elsewhere. It appears that the 'Sarah' left Port Wakefield with a cargo of wool for the 'Scottish Chief', and while alongside the ship Messrs. Cameron and Pickering went on board and were in conversation with the Captain. The cutter left the ship about 9 o'clock Wednesday morning.

The Adelaide Register - 21 October, 1862

THE FATAL ACCIDENT IN THE GULF

Mr. Campion has kindly furnished the following particulars:
On Wednesday, the 17th the cutter Sarah left the Wakefield with wool for the Scottish Chief at the anchorage about seven miles out. She discharged the same alongside, and left with seven persons on board, namely, the master of the cutter, William McKay, Peter Johnson, seaman (the two persons on whose remains the Inquest was recently held at Port Adelaide); Mr. John Pickering, sheep-farmer, who has left a wife and three children to lament his untimely death; his partner Mr. Angus Cameron; Mr. James Fox, late mounted trooper; Henry Nell, a friend of the master, and Henry Taylor, ostler at Mr. Campion's, who was on his way to town to enter Adelaide Hospital having sustained injuries by a fall from the 'Scottish Chief' to the gunwale of a small boat. The articles of female apparel mentioned at the Inquest were merely a bundle forwarded to a laundress at Port Adelaide.

In John Pickering's last letter he intimated that he would shortly be shearing his sheep, the wool to be shipped to England. Apparently this was what he was doing when he and his partner met their death.

According to James Potter of The Salisbury and District Historical Society, "The procedure for loading wheat or wool onto the ships for export overseas was a fairly involved and tedious task. At the time mentioned (1862) probably the only port in South Australia with wharfage facility would have been Port Adelaide. Elsewhere along the coastline the wool was transported in drays down to the sea shore and at low tide they were driven alongside the small boats (cutters or ketches) which were beached above the water level and the load transferred by hand from the dray to the cutter. The loading would be completed during the period of low tide while the drays could reach the boats on the dry beach. The boats would then wait for the tide to come in until the draft was deep enough when they would then sail out to the larger ships anchored in deeper water.

"The bales of wool would then be winched up from the cutter and loaded into the larger vessel. Each small boat would probably make one or two trips each 24 hours depending on the period of the tide. It might take a week or more to load the ship.

"Depending on the location and depths of water, the distance travelled by the cutter could be up to five miles from the beach. It was not usually considered all that hazardous although poor distribution of the load and rough weather sometimes caused trouble.

"On the particular occasion in October 1862, the 'Scottish Chief' loaded wool at Port Wakefield which is the northern point of St. Vincent Gulf and is about 50 miles (80km) north of Port Adelaide. It loaded 4,000 bales of wool which took about two and a half weeks.

"The cutter 'Sarah' was actually engaged in small coastal trading and had done a run from Port Adelaide to Port Wakefield with a general cargo of stores. After discharging her cargo she probably engaged for a couple of days in running wool out to the 'Scottish Chief'. On completion of the loading it appears she took on four passengers and set sail for Adelaide about 9a.m. on the Wednesday. It would have been about half way to Adelaide when she was struck by the violent storm and capsized and all was lost. Only two of the bodies were found."

The procedure for payment of the wool that was loaded onto the 'Scottish Chief' is not known to me, so did the money go down with their bodies, or was reimbursement given to Sarah his wife? Otherwise it would have been a devastating financial blow to all concerned.

The Adelaide Observer - Saturday 18 October 1862
MISCELLANEOUS

The Gale of Wednesday (extracts from report)
"Towards midday incessant flashes of vivid lightning and here and there the surface of the Gulf was agitated by flaws of wind. But it was later in the day that a whole hurricane came sweeping from about the West. In an instant the Gulf was lashed into foam.

"Verandahs around Port Adelaide were carried away and trees blown over. There had been nothing to surpass its violence for many years."

Here we must pause and take a look at the person who was with John Pickering on the boat, and who died the same tragic death - Angus Cameron. Who was he and why were they together?

The Bond for Angus Cameron, sheds some light on the mystery.

"Angus Cameron formerly of Point Prince, in Queens County, Prince Edward Island in British North America, and late of Port Wakefield, sheepfarmer, carrying on business in partnership with one John Pickering deceased. His goods, chattels, rights, credits and effects were assumed not to exceed £1000", whereas in John's case the sum of £2500 is given.

With the death of the partners, the partnership known as Pickering and Cameron, founded with the purchase of land in 1862 also died. And that should have brought the story of John Pickering to (another) close.

But the last letter had not sounded like an end, but a new beginning - full of hope and youthful optimism. How could my mind switch off and close the book? The end of a chapter no doubt, but certainly not the end of the story.

Chapter 5

Poor Sarah, a widow, with three children to care for, and all John's business interests to unravel and deal with. Did she ever look back and regret leaving England? John's promise of returning home when he considered he had made enough money must have rung in her ears many, many times.

In the space of a few short months she had lost her father, her youngest son, and now her husband. Fate had decreed that neither Sarah, the one who had suffered most from 'home fever', nor her family, would ever return to England.

A strong minded women she must have been: she had quickly become used to helping on the farm, making cheeses and butter, and running a store. As a child and young woman, living in a part of industrial England, it is possible that she had no training whatsoever for the life she would eventually lead, and this fact alone highlights her strength of character.

Notwithstanding the kind of problems she must have encountered in the next few months, on 7 April, 1863, Sarah Ann Pickering sold 35 square miles and 1301 acres, at Port Wakefield, to Charles Merrett of Kooringa (Land Record Memorial 132) for the sum of £1925.6.6d.

John had died intestate and this would doubtless have caused Sarah a great deal of stress. It is interesting to note that on the Bond, Joseph Kinsey, who had owned land near to John Pickering in Salisbury, now living at Pancharpoo, and Samuel Olley, farmer, of Riverton, acted as witnesses, together with John Tallack, Minister, of Saddleworth.

Joseph Kinsey was responsible for writing a memorial to Sarah on her death, and would therefore seem to have been a close friend of the family, maintaining links with them throughout their lives.

Joseph Kinsey (1820-1907) and Phoebe Kinsey, née Baker (1824-1906) came to South Australia in 1849 in the ship 'Samuel Boddington'. Accompanying them was their infant daughter, Martha, who was born in 1848 in Staffordshire, England. They settled at Salisbury where they remained for some years before moving to Steelton in 1857. Mr. Kinsey offered part of his section 1016 for the building site for the Pancharpoo Methodist Chapel, which was completed and opened on 1 August, 1858. The church was used for a school until 1864 and Mr. Kinsey became the school teacher, but relinquished this position in that year when the Steelton School was built. He returned to his trade of wheelwright as well as farming his two sections. During these years the family lived on the Pancharpoo section, but by 1884 he owned sections 329, 330 and 331.

Mr. Kinsey was a local preacher and great church worker at Pancharpoo. In 1892 he and his wife retired to Waterloo to live and on 20 February 1897 they celebrated their Golden Wedding. Phoebe Kinsey died in 1906 and Joseph in 1907. Both are buried in Pancharpoo Cemetery. John Pickering and Joseph Kinsey were the same age, came from Staffordshire, and were local preachers, arriving in South Australia in 1849; it seems quite possible they already knew each other in England.

We must now look closely at Sarah's position. Stranded in a country she did not call home, and responsible for the well being of three young children; an accumulation of business interests to deal with, money to be wisely spent and invested for the future, and suddenly no regular wage earner at her side. Her decision to sell all the farming activities at Port Wakefield was perhaps influenced by the size of the farm and to 'return to our old place to live', which was maybe the nearest place that Sarah could call home.

". . . under these trying circumstances Mrs. Pickering sold out and returned to her old home. This heavy affliction seemed to be borne with Christian resignation and submission." (Primitive Methodist Record - July 1885). The close knit chapel community at Pancharpoo, in which she had earlier played such a prominent part, would have supported her in her fight to recover and once again lead a normal life.

Although this land and property was still on lease to Charles Gladlow until 1866, it seems that provision was made for their accommodation, and there was none better to turn to for advice and comfort in her loss, than the Primitive Methodist Minister for the area, John Tallack.

In a brief synopsis of their lives contained within a report of Joseph John and Julia's Golden Wedding, we read: "when Sarah the widow and young family returned to Waterloo, they carried on wheat farming, but the seasons being rather bad, it meant a big struggle for them. Hay chaff at that time being £18.0.0d. a ton, they reaped their first crop by hand. Joseph John always got on well with the blacks around Waterloo, as generally speaking they were quiet, except when visited by a tribe from the Murray."

From information given by Dr. Arnold Hunt, Historical Society, of Uniting Church, South Australia, John Tallack came to Australia about 1830. As he died aged 52 years on 24 May, 1882, it would seem that he must have been a very young child on arrival. He entered the Ministry of the Primitive Methodist Church in 1860 and served at Mt. Barker for two years, which was evidently his first posting. He then served for two years from 1862-1864 at Pancharpoo (a rural circuit later called Saddleworth) and from 1864 to 1866 at Strathalbyn. He then is shown as assisting at Pancharpoo and Saddleworth for sixteen years, not then as an active minister but a farmer from 1865.

Fourteen months after John Pickering's tragic death, a report in the Register dated 2 January 1864 states, "30 December, 1863, at the Primitive Methodist Chapel, Beverley, by Rev. J.G. Wright, Rev. J. Tallack to Mrs. S. A. Pickering, both of the Light."

Sarah had taken the decision to marry again, probably to give all of them the security they needed, an arrangement that was normal in the nineteenth century both in England and Australia, at a time when a welfare state did not exist.

It must be noted here that John Tallack was also one of the first settlers in Steelton, and we learn from A History of the Steelton District, that "John Pickering's widow, Sarah Ann, remarried to John Tallack on 30th December 1863 and they continued to occupy the store at Kunden (Carlsruhe), (this would be on land section 1001). John Tallack was a carpenter and he made many fine pieces of furniture for the Steelton folk. He was also a local preacher and Sunday School Superintendent at Pancharpoo for many years. John and Sarah died in 1882 and 1885 respectively and were buried in Pancharpoo Cemetery.

Sarah Ann Tallack, formerly Pickering, née Sanders

At the time of their marriage, Sarah was 41 years of age and John Tallack 33 years of age. According to the law, on the day they married all Sarah's estate became his property.

There were no children from this union, but it is obvious from Joseph John's short letter, that his stepchildren thought very well of him. When John Tallack's new appointment was arranged, all the family moved with him, and this is where it could be that the children received some of their education. As Pancharpoo Church was used also as a school from 1858, it is quite likely that all the children received some education while living at Steelton, as Joseph John was well capable of writing a letter in May 1864 in a very well formed hand. He suggests that both Samuel Daniel and himself would remain at school in Strathalbyn for the next two years, which would make him sixteen years old, surely over the school leaving age for that period in history.

It would appear that the family were looking forward to the time spent in a town, rather than in the bush "which would afford us many advantages".

However, the conclusion of John Tallack's appointment in Strathalbyn in 1866, seems to have coincided with the termination of the lease of the farm at The Light, because in 1866 the family moved back to Steelton.

Did John Tallack make a conscious decision to leave the ministry and concentrate on being a farmer? There seems to have been a compromise, as he is shown as a farmer and assisting Minister at Pancharpoo and Saddleworth until his death in 1882.

According to the Primitive Methodist Record of July 1885, "Mr. Tallack's health failing, he left the ministry, and the family once more returned to their old home." This information, gleaned from a memorial to Sarah perhaps gives a better indication as to why the decision was made to return to 'the bush'.

So, in 1866 they returned to Steelton to make a permanent home for the family. Joseph John was sixteen years of age, educated to some degree, and would be of enormous help on the farm, having spent most of his young life helping his father. Samuel Daniel, at eleven years of age would also be of considerable help, and eight years old Sarah Jane would be good company for her mother.

The letters home either ceased or were not kept by any member of the family, so the lifestyle is now left to the imagination, helped by information gleaned from other sources. It was clear from the last letter that the children were happy with Sarah's choice of husband, and happily accepted him as their stepfather. All would have been expected to help on the farm, but with John's health failing, the biggest load would have fallen on Joseph John's shoulders.

Questions remained: what happened to the three children? Would farming still play a part in their lives? Would there be any desire or opportunity left to return to England? Would prosperity continue, and if there were any descendants, what kind of lives would they lead? Would the land they originally owned remain in the family? Could there still be a point of contact?

These and many more questions filled my curious mind, and combined with the dogged persistence required to have got this far, drove me mercilessly onwards.

Chapter 6

At the very beginning of my research, I heard from the South Australian Heraldry and Genealogy Society that John Joseph Pickering had died on 1 March 1937 aged 87 years and Julia Pickering had died on 28 June 1938 aged 87 years and both were buried at Overland Corner There was no absolute proof that these people were part of the family for which I was searching, but it did sound promising, and was a starting point for further research. Further correspondence from SAGHS stated: "Also found were some land records relating to John Joseph Pickering, but have not looked them all up. One related to a block of land he owned, at the time he died, at Yacka, about 40 miles north of Port Wakefield. He had owned this land for just over 30 years. There are also some land records relating to Samuel Daniel Pickering, in the Hundred of Waterloo (therefore in the area somewhere near Port Wakefield), but apart from that I haven't found anything else about him .... The index to marriages from 1889 to 1906 has not yet been released... So far the only one [of John Pickering's children] that I know married is John Joseph, though I don't know when. As yet I have also been unable to establish whether there are any descendants of John Pickering in Australia. I tried to get John Joseph's will, but there isn't one. So far all indications with him are that he did not have any children."

This was the familiar 'dead end'. It seemed that descendants, if any at all, would be few and far between, and it was at this stage that I decided to admit defeat, put all the research at the back of a cupboard, and forget all about it.

John Pickering's spirit, however, was having none of it, and after a couple of years, one of quite a few strange, unexpected coincidences occurred.

106

Chapter 7

We were on holiday in Cornwall, and decided to make a day trip to Fowey. After doing all the usual things day trippers do on a lovely hot, sunny day, we all decided to seek some refreshment, and wandered into the village, pottering around the shops as we went along. My eyes were drawn to a bookshop, where, in a small display in one corner of the window was The Cornish Miner in Australia, or Cousin Jack Down Under by Phillip J. Payton. I was vaguely curious about which part of Australia it referred to, and decided to go into the shop and find out.

The inside front cover of the book confirmed that the area was South Australia, so I opened it at random and the first thing that caught my eye was the name Rev. J. G. Wright. Places leapt out at me: Kooringa - the post mark on one of the envelopes of the letters - Wallaroo, Burra Burra. Suddenly, from being just an idle pastime, my research took on a different meaning. They were real places and real people with their own history, interesting enough to prompt someone to do serious research. Mention was made of a diary written by Rev. J. G .Wright.

I was so elated and excited that the owner of the bookshop became curious and I had to explain to him why I was in such a state, and he became just as intrigued, and told me that the book had only just been published. Of course I purchased it on the spot, leaving the shop waving it in the air, to the puzzlement of my returning family. The candle had been rekindled, and was burning brighter than ever before.

On my return from holiday, I immediately wrote another letter to

SAGHS asking for details of Rev. J.G. Wright and his diary. Their reply gave some details of the man, nothing on the diary, but also enclosed was a photocopy from the Society's Jubilee 150 publication Biographical Index of South Australians 1836-1885 covering the Pickering name.

PICKERING Joseph John   par: John and Sarah Ann b: 1850 d: 1.3.1937 Bd: Overland Corner SA occ: Farmer, Grazier re: Overland Corner, Parcoola M: Julia née BATT b: c1851 d: 28.6.1938 ch: Angus Cameron (1879), Bertram Saunders (1880), Sarah Sylvia (1883), Joseph Edmund (1884), Saml. Allen (1894), 6 others.

Another piece in the jigsaw. I could not believe my luck - a three year wait had been rewarded. The details fitted perfectly, and I was intrigued to see that Joseph John had a son named Angus Cameron. It had got to be the right family. No children indeed! Only a family of eleven! Surely I could feel reasonably certain that descendants still existed in South Australia - and they were going to be found! But how? Having had no formal training in genealogy, I was out of my depth. All I had was enthusiasm, and I was floundering.

Help very often comes from unexpected quarters, and not always in a recognisable form. A working colleague 'just happened' to have a cousin living in Victoria to whom she regularly wrote, and on hearing my story, told him all about it. He was just as intrigued and wanted to help, but all he could suggest was to look in the telephone directory for South Australia. He sent me a list of nine names taken from the directory in the Salisbury area he thought might be relevant.

As the Pickering family's last address was in 1864 in Strathalbyn, it seemed like a mighty long shot and I disregarded these nine names for a long time, feeling that the chance of success was so slight as to be of no use. However, after having no results from other sources, and beginning to feel very desperate, I decided that nothing, apart from a small amount of postage, would be lost in following this course of action.

I carefully composed a letter, giving details of the family I was seeking, assurances of a genuine interest, together with references should the recipient wish to check my authenticity and I sent this letter to seven of the nine addresses. I had three very prompt replies, but none of them connected in any way. However, one lady wrote, "unfortunately we are not the Pickerings you are looking for - but by a strange coincidence (I started to feel excited) I went to school with a family of Pickerings who lived in the vicinity of Overland Corner who may be able to help you."

Overland Corner is many miles away from Salisbury, but sounded promising, and the two addresses were for Barmera - again miles away. Off went two more letters and in November of that year a letter plopped onto the mat with a Barmera postmark. With fingers and toes crossed I hardly dared open it. On reading it, I knew instantly what it must feel like to win the lottery.

"Thank you for your interest in the Pickering family tree. Joseph John was my husband's grandfather. My husband's name is Leo Foster Pickering, son of Douglas Foster Pickering who lived at Overland Corner. However, I am forwarding your letter to (Mrs) Irma McGregor, daughter of Douglas Foster. She resides in Adelaide, South Australia, where she should be able to acquire more

information on the Pickering family, and you should receive a letter
from her sometime in the future. Thanking you for your letter.
(Mrs) Shirley Pickering

We celebrated with a bottle of champagne. However, I was
cautious: there was no address, and everything now hinged on a
reply.

Irma McGregor, bless her, came up with the goods in magnificent
fashion, and has worked away at the family ever since to get them
to sort out all their details up to the present, and the following
continuation of the story was made possible mainly by Irma's hard
work, together with some professional help from Andrew Peake.

Another quotation from Steelton District History - "Farms in the
early days were family concerns with all the sons and daughters
living at home until married. Unmarried men and women tended to
remain in the family home and helped to look after their nieces and
nephews and elderly parents. One son from each family usually
inherited the main property and other sons, when possible, bought,
with family assistance, a farm nearby.   Some left the district
altogether and sought other employment. Many did casual work,
labouring, fencing, gardening, clearing timber, chopping wood,
hoeing thistles and other various tasks.

"Most people took a pride in their farms and household duties and
there was little time for outside entertainments. The simple life was
a satisfying way of life to the Steelton folk and their churches were
the centre of their social life. However, in this small community
friendship between neighbours was a source of pleasure and when
time allowed visits were made to each others farms. Singsongs
around pianos or organs were enjoyed and the population went

where their horses would take them, which limited their travels.
"As a school had been built in 1864 for the Steelton children, the
Pancharpoo Chapel was no longer needed in that respect, and it
was decided in 1866 to enlarge the building. For this purpose donations of money and labour were given by:-

Mr. & Mrs. Abrahams	Mr Brown
Mr. Blackaby	Mrs Baillie
Mrs. Buchanan	Mr Davidson
Miss Edgebe	Mr Golding
Miss P. Harper	Mr Hazel
Miss Holder	Mr Howe
Mrs. Hunt	Mr & Mrs Ianson
Mr Matthias Paxton	Mr Phillips
Mr. Ivett	Mr Rogers
Mr. J. Jones	Mr Rollins
Mr. Kinsey	Mr Steele
Mr & Mrs Martin	Mr Stephens
Mr. D. McFeat	Mr P. Scott
Mr. W. McFeat	Mr & Mrs Tallack
Mr. Nourse	Mr Watts
Mr. Olley	Mr Wayland
Mr & Mrs Prior	Mr S. Webb
Mr. Parken	Rev. G. Wright

"Mr. John Tallack was a carpenter but he also appears to be the
mason in charge of the building. He was also the Sunday School
Superintendent from 1866 to 1870 when existing records cease.
Mr. Tallack was a lay preacher and performed burials from 1867
until May 1882 shortly before his death.

"A report of the re-opening of Pancharpoo Chapel was included in the March 9th edition of the Supplement to the South Australian Weekly Chronicle and Mail, 1867. It reads as follows:-

On Sunday the Primitive Methodist Chapel at Pancharpoo was re-opened, having been closed for some months for enlargement and repair. Three sermons were preached by the Rev. J. S. Wayland. On Monday a tea meeting was held, which was well attended, and the collections liberal. Mr. J. Tallack acted as chairman at the public meeting, which was addressed by Messrs. Wayland, Goods, Willshire, Kinsey and Olley. The report stated that labour to the value of £74.0.0d. had been given, and that after the receipt of the collections, the tea and the proceeds of a fruit stall, there would be a deficiency of nearly £200.0.0d. including a debt on the old chapel.

Extracts from the Pancharpoo Sunday School records show:

John Pickering	Dec 1859-Jan 1860. Teacher 1870
Joseph John Pickering	Sept 1860-61,1865-66 Teacher 1866-70
Samuel Pickering	Sep 1860, Teacher Oct 1861, 1865-70
Sarah Ann Pickering	July 1861, 1865-66-68
Sarah Jane Pickering	July 1866-67-69-70

Sarah Jane was for many years an organist at Pancharpoo Chapel, carrying with her a portable organ. This reflects the way in which the family once more integrated itself into the life of the Steelton community.

The population of Steelton were not all Methodists: there were at least a dozen Irish Catholic families among the first settlers and

Sarah Jane Pickering

112

they probably held services in private homes before the Catholic Church was built at Marrabel in 1867. There were also a number of Lutheran migrants in the area and two miles to the north a church was built in 1863-64 on land belonging to Carl Ahrns, and the area was named Carlsruhe.

Pancharpoo Chapel Account Book - Disboursement 7 Jun 1860			
Paling	£3.15. 0	To J.B.Miller	£4.15. 0
Nails	7. 9	J.Kinsey	2. 0. 0
Bricks	1. 5. 0	Paling	15. 6
To J.B.Miller	2. 0. 0	Paid back to Circuit	
To Mr Lambert	2. 0. 0	Comm.	3. 8. 4
Mr Kinsey	1. 0. 0	Cober for ceiling	10. 0
Locks	8. 6	Painting & Fitting	
		Door etc.	4. 0
		Total	£22. 9. 1

Three days after his 24th birthday, on 22 October, 1873, Joseph John, bachelor, married Julia Foster, spinster, aged 22 years, at the Primitive Methodist Church, Auburn, in the district of Upper Wakefield. Residence at the time of marriage was Pancharpoo, and both fathers, John Pickering and Edmund Foster, were recorded as deceased. Joseph John's occupation was given as farmer, Julia at that time having no occupation. The ceremony was performed by Stephen Wellington, officiating minister at Saddleworth, and was witnessed by Samuel Long, bootmaker, from Auburn, and somebody from Pancharpoo.

Julia was the daughter of Edmund Foster, a grocer, and Charlotte

Allen, both from Wotton in Surrey, England. They married at Wotton on 13 March, 1850 by licence in the Church of England by William J. Edlin. James Foster, Edmund's father was a bailiff, and Charlotte's father, Thomas Henry, was a tradesman.

According to a newspaper report of John and Julia's Golden Wedding, Julia was three years old when she arrived in Australia, having been born on 15 May, 1851. Information within the family has it that her mother Charlotte 'was lady in waiting for Lord and Lady Green' and she married the butler and lived on the estate. Three years after their marriage he died of pneumonia and she married William Batts, a mason, and settled in Auburn". This family story has yet to be proved.

William Batts and family came to live in Steelton as early as 1861 their children's names appearing in the Sunday School records in July of that year. They were Julia, Edith, Eliza, Elsie and William. The family had their share of tragedy when on 23 March, 1868 Edith fell from her horse and was dragged, with her foot in the stirrup. The horse panicked and would not stop running: she died from her injuries.

Their only son William was helping to thatch the roof of the shed, or barn, and his job was to be inside to get the string and pass it through again, as the thatch was tied on with string threaded through a needle. He fell and was killed as a result.

"After a few years, Julia's stepfather took up land at Steelton and started farming. Julia could never forget the first ploughing they did, she had to lead the two horses in a single furrow plough, and of course got into many a scrape for not keeping them straight. She was very fond of reading, especially history, and as a young woman she would read till early hours of the morning. When not allowed on some occasions the precious oil, she would sit by the window and read by the aid of the moon.

114

"She lived at Steelton until she was married." (Golden Wedding newspaper report

On 2nd January 1875 at Steelton, Julia gave birth to their first child, a daughter whom they christened Edith. This could have been a special token of remembrance to the sister she had so tragically lost.

Eighteen months later, on 18 June 1876, a son was born and named John George. During the early part of 1877 Julia again was pregnant and on 29 November 1877 another daughter, Amelia, was born.

The land in its early stages yielded well but because no superphosphate was used it degenerated over the years and by 1890 the farmers were finding it difficult to produce enough grain to make progress. This was also due in some part to the prolonged drought in the 1880s which ended in January 1889 with heavy summer rains.

The Chronicle dated 19 January 1867 reported: "Steelton had a thunderstorm, the road was three foot under water, the schoolmaster's house was flooded and the cellar of Mr. Martin's store was flooded."

The coming of superphosphate at this time revolutionised the crop yield and where they had got down to bushels an acre it became bags. In those days 4-bushel bags were used and quite a few acres of the crops were cut for hay to feed the horse teams.

It is known that Joseph John and Julia moved to a farm at Yacka during 1877, before or after the birth of Amelia is not known. As the family was rapidly expanding, and the land was not as fertile as in earlier years, perhaps these factors influenced the decision to move away.

Of course, this would reduce the workforce on the land for Sarah, but by this time Samuel Daniel would be 22 years old and Sarah Jane 19 years of age. Nevertheless, Joseph John would be greatly

115

missed by all the family.

The first child to be born at Yacka on 10 June 1879 was a son, Angus Cameron. It causes great curiosity as to why this name was chosen. Joseph John was little more than a child when his father's tragic accident occurred, but it must have had a lasting effect on his life. Had he grown fond of his father's business partner? To name one of his sons after him was perhaps some kind of tribute and a memorial to his name.

Another son, Bertram Saunders, was born on 17 December 1880, this time Sarah Ann's maiden name being used.

Joseph John kept a notebook and items from it give an idea of their lifestyle.

In 1876 a mowing and horse rake cost him £4.10.0d. while a spotted heifer brought £6.15.0d. The following year he sold eight steers to a Mr. Goode for £49.10.0d. and John Daly paid Joseph 6d. a week to graze a cow on his paddock, and one shilling for a mare.

John Cary worked for Mr. Pickering in 1879, being paid £1 per week, and whilst employed ran up the following account to his employer:

Cash to go to hospital	£2. 0.0
1/4 lb of tobacco	1.3
1 doz matches	0.6
1 bottle rum	4.0
1 pair boots	16. 6
1 pipe cover	0. 3
2 sticks of tobacco	0. 6

In the same year William Fisher was employed at 10s a week and obtained the following from his employer:

1 pair boots	16. 6
1 hat	5. 9
6 x 3d soaps	1. 6
1 pair moles	7. 6
1 vest	7. 6
1 file	1. 4

William's priorities seem to have been different from John's. At that time, also, John Edwards, a carter, was paid threepence a bushel to cart 635 bushels of wheat - £7. 18. 9

In 1882 Fred Fielder paid 10s a week to board with the Pickerings, and amongst other things paid Mr. Pickering 4s 6d. for an axe and 1s. for an axe handle. He also ran up 5s.0d on the barber's account. In that year also Mr. Pickering did some dealing, selling to S.H. Pelton, four horses and their harnesses, three cows and a spring cart. Later that year he hired them all back at £1 a week.

In 1884 he paid £1 to someone for digging a grave and the following year he did some ploughing for a neighbour, receiving 7.6d. an acre.*

Sarah was now a grandmother five times over, and her life seemed settled, but it soon took another turn, when on 24 May 1882, her second husband, John Tallack, died aged 52 years and was buried at Pancharpoo. This event would have turned everyone's life upside down, as, of course, all the land, property and money had reverted to him on his marriage to Sarah, according to the law at that time.

Surprisingly his will had been made on 11 December 1867. Was his health failing to the extent that he deemed it prudent to make a will so soon after moving back to Steelton, at the age of only 37

*History of Overland Corner and its Hotel

117

years? It revealed a scrupulously fair deal for everyone in the family, bequeathing everything to his wife Sarah Ann 'for her natural life' and 'all and everything which remains shall be equally divided between my wife's three children.' He appointed Sarah sole executrix of the will and it was witnessed by James S. Wayland, Minister, and Sampson Webb. This was proved and registered in the Supreme Court by Sarah on 15 July 1882. Sarah was a widow again, with a farm to look after, but not single handed, as Samuel Daniel and Sarah Jane were still living at home and presumably helping with the farm.

At the time of John Tallack's death, Julia was two months pregnant with her sixth child, and on 25 March 1883 a daughter, Sarah Sylvia, was born and their seventh child, a son, Joseph Edmund, was born on 24 October, 1884

1885 brought with it a great deal of sadness, for on 30 April 1885 Sarah died aged 63 years and was buried with her second husband John Tallack at Pancharpoo Cemetery.

The grave of John Tallack and Sarah Ann Pickering -Tallack in the cemetery of Pancharpoo Primitive Methodist Church (Plot 44)

118

The Pancharpoo Cemetery which is located to the east of Pancharpoo Church seems to have been in use from 1865 for on 16 October 1865 Mr. Joseph Kinsey was paid the sum of £3.0 0d. for the burying ground and the first burial registered in the Cemetery Book was that of John Baillie who died on 27 February, 1865.

Of the Pickering-Tallack family, only Sarah Ann and John Tallack are buried there. Sarah Ann's youngest son, George Wright, had died too early to have been buried in the cemetery and the

Summerhill Farm - renamed Talla Walla (photo Ervyn Behn)

whereabouts of his last resting place are unknown. However, a headstone was found in the floor of Ervyn Behn's stable bearing the inscription 'G.W.Pickering, who died April 17th 1861 aged 13 months'.

In the Memorial written in the Primitive Methodist Record for July 1885, by Joseph Kinsey, the last paragraph paints an illuminating picture. "In March last, some changes took place in the family, which perhaps, gave a little anxiety and extra work, together with a severe cold which brought diarrhea (sic) which, in

Headstone dug up from the Talla Walla
stable

119

the space of three weeks carried her through the gates of death to her final abode. Aged 63, Sarah had been a member of the Primitive Methodist Church for 40 years."

Obviously, "change in the family giving a little anxiety and causing extra work" was a very diplomatic way of expressing a delicate situation. What could it mean?

Looking at the records, it is interesting to note that 'in March last' - the 25th to be precise - Sarah Jane Pickering was married at Steelton to Jeremiah Jones. Had there been a family row? Did Sarah not approve of Sarah's choice of husband? Or had this marriage got nothing to do with the cause of the anxiety?

Jeremiah Jones senior (1829-1907), Sarah Jane's father-in-law, had come from the County of Kilkenny, Ireland, on the 'John Knox', landing at Point Henry (Geelong) on 14 July, 1851. Jeremiah met his wife, Anne Mitchell, (1829-1871) on board ship on the way to Australia. They were married in Victoria and went to the goldfields at Ballarat, where they were fortunate to strike gold, enabling them to purchase land at Steelton in 1855 and settled on section 1028, where he built a three roomed house. Jeremiah also owned sections 42,62,63 & 1031 which he farmed until 1868 when he sold his property to Heinrich C.J. Schmaal and shifted to Bagot's Well. Although the Jones family attended Pancharpoo Chapel while at Steelton they were Anglicans and were members of St. Phillip's Church of England at Belvidere, near Marrabel. Anne Jones died in 1871 and she and four children, John, Ann, Annie Jane and Francis Thomas are buried in the Belvidere Cemetery, the children having all died in infancy. Three children survived into adulthood: Samuel, Jeremiah and Robert. Jeremiah married a second time to Eliza Davison (1841-1888) on 20 December, 1871, at Marrabel. Eliza was the daughter of Robert and Jane Davison of Marrabel.

120

Jeremiah and Eliza had two children. Following the death of Eliza in 1888 at the age of 47 years, Jeremiah shifted from Bagot's Well to Yacka in 1892 where he died in 1907 aged 78 years. For many years he was a member of Kapunda Council and in politics as a freetrader. He and Eliza are both buried at Belvidere. The property at Yacka, 'Sunny Braes', is still farmed by Jeremiah's descendants.

As Jeremiah junior was a farmer, working on his father's farm at Yacka, it is possible that Sarah Jane's brother Joseph John had played cupid, although both families must have known one another well from living at Steelton in the past. It seems probable that this union caused a violent reaction as far as Sarah Ann was concerned, enough to disrupt the family life as they knew it, and ended with Sarah's death.

On 14 August 1885, Samuel Daniel was granted Letters of Administration and was given six calendar months to settle the terms of the will which his mother had only partly dealt with, and was sworn under £600.0.0d. As the estate was to be divided equally into three parts, was the farm to be sold, so that all three children received the money from the proceeds? If so, would that leave Samuel Daniel without a home? Could he afford to buy out his brother and sister?

Was the sale of Summerhill Farm (Sections 323 and 327), started prior to April 1860, ever completed? John had said in his last letter that it was being purchased over a six year period and John had met his death in 1862. The family had returned to the house and store on sections 1001/1002 and this was still being farmed by Samuel Daniel after his mother's death, together with 323 and 327 (Summerhill Farm) according to a local historian. He also farmed land sections 326 and 1005 adjacent to their own land owned by Joseph Kinsey and sections 1011 and 1008 belonging to William and David McFeat, another near neighbour. However, it is thought

121

that he sold up and left the district in 1887. As it is known that he owned land (sections 393,399,400/1, 154/5/6) in the Waterloo area perhaps this is where he moved to after the sale of land at Steelton.

Gottlieb Behn, a farmer in Steelton, settled his son Wilhelm on Summerhill Farm in the 1880s, which could mean that it was purchased direct from Samuel Daniel. This farm, renamed 'Talla Walla', is still being farmed by the Behn family, and is where the gravestone was found.

Eleven months after their marriage, and living at Yacka, Sarah Jane gave birth to her first born. On 14 March 1886 a son, Robert Mitchell, was born.

The following year there were two births to celebrate, on 9 July 1887, Joseph John and Julia had their eighth child, a son, Douglas Foster, and on 27 July 1887 Sarah and Jeremiah had a second son, Jeremiah Bruce.

It was three years before another child was born to Joseph John and Julia, and on 24 June 1890 a girl, Julia Vida, arrived, but in the previous year on 25 February 1889 Sarah and Jeremiah had had a third son, Joseph Maurice.

The two families had settled at Yacka, the Pickering family with nine children, and the Jones family with three. However, the Jones family decided to move to Salters Springs, and their fourth son was born there on 7 November, 1890. They named him Samuel Pickering Jones, and on 15 September, 1892, still at Salters Springs, their fifth child and first daughter, Sarah Winifred was born.

By this time, Joseph John and Julia's eldest child, Edith, was seventeen years old, and still at home, but over the Christmas period gave them some news which could have upset all the family. Edith was pregnant. What kind of reaction occurred we shall never know, and what decisions were reached can only be gauged by one single fact.

On 20 June 1893 she gave birth to a daughter, Daisy Elfreda, who was adopted by Joseph John and Julia and brought up as their own child.

Edith Butler, née Pickering, 1948

There had been no addition to Joseph John and Julia's family since 1890, so perhaps they thought they had finished having children, and Edith's child could be the youngest of the large family. However, 1894 brought two new additions for on 19th June 1894 to Sarah and Jeremiah, now living at Dalkey, another son was born and called William Rossiter, and Joseph John and Julia's last child, just before Christmas - on 18 December 1894 - a son, Samuel Allen.

Edith, at 19 years of age, left home and went to Milang to work for people called "Dunk" and then Mathers at Strathalbyn. She married John Butler on 11 December 1895. He worked for Rankines at Angas Plains and delivered wheat to Milang. During the course of the next 23 years they also had a large family of nine children five boys and four girls.

Meanwhile, during 1897, Joseph John and Julia, together with all their family, with the exception of Edith, made the decision to move. What inspired that decision is a matter of conjecture, maybe there was a drought of a bad harvest, but whatever the reason, the land at Yacka still belonged to Joseph John when he died, and had owned the land for just over fifty years.

"They set out with two bullock teams carrying all their possessions, for Overland Corner, River Murray, to open up the Mallee Scrub. It was a long and tedious journey and Julia was suffering from an attack of influenza and it was feared more than once she would not live to see the journey out, but she managed to pull through safely. They arrived at what is known as Devlin's Pound about eight miles below Overland Corner on Christmas Eve of 1897, where they spent their first Christmas Day on the River Murray (Information from report of Golden Wedding report).

They made their home at Parcoola Station homestead built by "Knobby" White. this had a great fence around it, fitted with loopholes so that the "marauding Aborigines" could be warded off. (Information from Irma McGregor)

Still at Dalkey, Sarah Jane and Jeremiah had their seventh child, another boy, on 14 June 1896, named Hartley Clifford. They then moved to Port Wakefield and on 16 July 1898 yet another son, Elliott Allan, was born.

On the move again, this time to Balaklava, and on 17 July 1900 their last child, and only second girl, Jane Gertrude, arrived. Sarah was by this time 42 years old and had a family of nine children, and Julia was 43 years of age when she gave birth to her tenth child.

Both women must have enjoyed very good health, because apart from repeatedly giving birth, and looking after extremely large families, they would still have been expected to do their share of the work on their farm.

"Joseph John and Julia were amongst the first wheat farmers in the region, but rabbits ate them out, but a good (?) Government let them have netting on long and easy terms" (quoted from a letter from Gwen Masters)

Another item from Joseph John's note book states:-

124

Mr. W. Brand's horse hired Nov.21st 1899 at l0.0d. per week. 1899 H. Starr worked 14 weeks at £1.0.0d. a week. 1899: Started reaping Nov 22nd. Finished Jan 8th 1900.

In 1903 he had nine paddocks of wheat totalling 203 acres. He provided wood for the steamers, employing men to cut and cart it from the scrub to the river bank, and sold at between 2.0d. and 6.0d. a ton (1.02 tonnes). In 1902 for a while H. King's boats were collecting from five to ten tons of wood each every few days. The main steamers supplied from 1901-1904 were 'The Ruby', 'Gem, 'Corowa' with 'The Princes Royal,' 'Struggler', 'Federal' and 'Alpha' calling occasionally. Also, in 1901 the 'Garra', 'Mannum' and 'Sapphire'.

In 1903 P. Eastwood would cart two lots of one ton loads of five feet lengths to the Parcoola pile. Joseph John paid l.9d. a ton for 5ft lengths and l.6d. a ton for 3 ft.6ins. lengths. 'The Federal' paid him 3.6d. a ton and the 'Alpha' 3.0d. a ton. He worked an exchange business with 'The Federal' in 1903 which took its loads in two ton lots, paying for it with. supplies.

Some steamers were floating shops. On 24 July 1903 a bag of flour was sold at £1.7.6d. In 1904 Joseph John bought many items from the boats, including an axe at 5 .3d., tobacco at 2.3d.a pound, tea at 8d.a half pound, butter at l0d.a lb. and blue nobs at a penny each. Sugar was 1.6d. for six pounds and potatoes cost 1.3d. a quarter hundredweight. The family also included sheep and cattle grazing in its pursuits. (extracted from *History of Overland Corner*).

Irma recollects that her father, Douglas Foster Pickering, Joseph John and Julia's eighth child, who was nine years old when the family moved to Parcoola, never had any more schooling, although his mother Julia was a former school teacher. This perhaps applied to the other children as well; apparently, they were too tired after cutting wood for the river steamers and clearing land. However, Julia Vida, their ninth child, four years old when arriving at Parcoola, received some of her schooling at Wistow while staying with her older sister Edith, and then spent her life, up to the age of 31, at Parcoola.

Parcoola as it was

Parcoola in 1988

Joseph John and Julia made friends wherever they went being possessed of a very hospitable nature. They were well known along the River and there was some very enjoyable times spent at their home where any who cared to come were always made welcome (Golden Wedding Report)

Joseph John used to play the piano and Julia sang and played. Many evenings and weekends were spent with friends and relatives as guests, and the girls would bake all day Friday for the weekends.

The homestead was made out of stone with a verandah overlooking a large garden, with the River Murray at the bottom of the garden. There were large stables and sheds belonging to Parcoola, the sheds having straw roofs. The boys slept in a shed away from the house and got out of bed before daylight to feed the horses and then harness them ready for work.

Douglas Foster Pickering and son-in-law making a haystack

The girls milked a herd of cows and Julia Vida often spoke of how on Monday mornings, her sister Daisy and she used to gather all the dirty clothes, and go down to the river bank and boil the copper, and do the washing by hand. Fishing was easy.

As the children grew older, their social life expanded and Bertram, who could play the accordion, walked or went by horse cart, driving for miles to play at dances. Angus could find his way home by the stars at night, travelling through miles of trees. He also swam the River Murray and led his horse across to go dancing.

In 1908, the minutes of a Sports Day Meeting held on 11 July, mention many of the leading lights of that time. It was proposed that the Sports be held on 12 September, and included on the

Committee was Angus Cameron Pickering, and amongst the judges
for that day were Joseph John and Angus Cameron Pickering.

On 13 December, 1905, at the age of 28 years, Amelia, more
commonly known as Dottie, and third child in the family, drowned
in the river. No details are known about this incident, and Irma
never remembers her father Douglas mentioning her. Certainly
whatever the reason, great distress would be felt by all at Parcoola.

Then came the First World War. Australia was far enough away
from the action, but ties with the mother country were still strong
enough for young Australian men to feel it their duty to 'do their
bit', and the boys in the Pickering family were no different, their
youngest child Samuel Allen, 20 years old at the outbreak of war,
volunteering for service, and fortunately surviving to come back
home and settle down with a wife and child.

Angus Cameron had never married and had stayed at home,
together with Joseph Edmund, to help their parents 'while others
passed on.' Angus, older than Samuel Allen by fifteen years, also

Pte.2227 Samuel Allen

Pte. 7538 Angus Cameron

128

felt duty bound to 'do his bit' and followed Samuel in 1917, and this is his story:

Nothing previously in Angus Cameron's life could have prepared him for what was to follow - after swearing on Oath, he enlisted on 14 July 1917 after being considered fit for service. His certificate of Medical Examination dated 12 July, 1917 listed him as 37 years of age 5'7" tall, with a chest measurement of 38", and a light complexion with grey eyes and brown hair; he was by trade a farmer and his religion was Church of England.

On 30 October, 1917 he travelled to Melbourne to join the ship 'Aeneas' and arrived in Devonport, England on 27 December, 1917 and from there to Sutton Veny to do his training. It would seem that the long sea voyage had not suited him because on 30 December 1917 he was admitted 'sick' to SuttonVeny Hospital where he stayed until 13 January 1918. On 1 April, 1918 after three months training, his battalion left Dover for Calais and on 9 April, 1918 proceeded to his unit.

Active service for Angus lasted for less than three months, and with the war drawing to its end, he was killed in action on 29 June, 1918. His body was buried in Shazelle Military Cemetery by Chaplain Rev. H. A. Hayden.

Following the instructions of the Will he had made such a short time previously, when signing for service, his effects were forwarded to his mother in a sealed parcel, and contained Notebook, Religious Book, Wallet, Keys, Fountain Pen, Cards, Photos, Postage Stamps, Disc (blank), Coin, and a German Button!

His death must have had a profound effect on Joseph John and Julia, removed as they were from the horrors of war, and a letter written by Joseph John to "The Officer in Charge, Base Records, Melbourne, Victoria," dated 18 July, 1918, from Wattle Street, Fullarton reads:

Dear Sir,
I received a cable from the Military authorities abroad reporting the death of my son, late Private Angus C. Pickering No. 7538 tenth battalion, killed in action in France. His late address was Overland Corner, River Murray. I would esteem it a great favor on your behalf if you would supply me with particulars to the best of your knowledge relating to his death etc. Thanking you in anticipation of an early reply.
The reply to that letter is not known, but on 18 September 1918, from Overland Corner, another letter was sent to Major Lean:
Your letter of July 25th to hand should have written before but have been very unwell and was under the Dr. hands for 2 weeks. My son was only away 8 months when news came of his death. It was the first time he ever left home I can hardly realise that he has gone. Will you kindly send me 2 certificates of No.7538 Private A. C. Pickerings 10th Battalion death and also any particulars of how he met his death if any should come to hand. Thanking you for your kindness,
Yours sincerely
Julia Pickering

P.S. One Certificate for the insurance office and one for the public trustee.

A reply was received because on 18 December 1918, from Overland Corner to Major Lean she wrote:

Thank you so much for your kind letter about my son A.C. Pickering. I would like to have a photo of his grave also to know that his grave was taken care of. He never left home before till he enlisted, his youngest brother had gone so he said he thought it was his duty to go and do his bit. It was a great shock to me when I heard of his death but I am not the only mother that has lost their dearest one. Thanking you for the certificates you sent and your last letter;

Yours sincerely,
Mrs. J Pickering

A further letter from Overland Corner, 10th May, 1920:

Your letter of April 23rd to hand advising me of the reburial of my son No. 5738 Private A. C. Pickering in Outtersteene Cemetery. Many thanks for your kind letter also for all your kind letters during my son's service in France and Belgium. Like a lot of Australian mothers I still miss my boy

Yours respectfully
Julia V. Pickering

And again from Overland Corner on 16th June, 1921:

Your letter to hand about next of kin to No. 7538 Private A.C. Pickering, his father Joseph John Pickering is living at Overland Corner South Australia we are farming here. My deceased son was not married he worked home on the farm until he enlisted. Thanking you and the Military Department for your kindness to us in our sad bereavement

Remain yours sincerely
Julia Pickering

Joseph John and Julia were then sent a pamphlet *Where the Australians Rest,* a duplicate photo of his grave, a British War Medal, a Victory Medal, a Memorial Scroll, and in 1922 a Memorial plaque. Even as late as September 1925 there was correspondence from the Australian Imperial Force stating that the body had been exhumed and re-interred in Outtersteene Communal Cemetery Extension, two and a half miles South West of Bailleul.

Two men with the name of Angus Cameron, both meeting their death in unfortunate circumstances, in the prime of their lives: truth is indeed stranger than fiction.

Joseph John and Julia must have had very heavy hearts. All their children had reached adulthood, something very rare during those times. All must have been made of strong material, and apart from Amelia, they were not as familiar with death as a good many other families who had to live this very harsh existence. Julia had survived ten births, and a long journey moving from Yacka to Parcoola when she nearly died. She had pulled through and her natural resilience and strong constitution must have stood her in good stead at this sad time.

The letter from Joseph John to 'The Officer in Charge Base Records', Melbourne dated 18 July 1918 gives the address as Wattle Street, Fullarton. Although nothing much as yet is known about Joseph's brother, Samuel Daniel, we do know that at some time he lived at 52 Wattle Street, Fullarton, which seems to suggest that both Joseph John and Julia sought comfort with him. They were back at Overland Corner in September of that year, when Julia stated "have been very unwell and was under the Doctor's hands for two weeks." Obviously the news had deeply upset them, but their courage in the face of this tragedy comes shining through in their letters. Always polite, no sign of bitterness, and with childlike gratitude for any help gratitude for any help received.

On 23 May, 1923 they finally received Angus Cameron's medals, and on 29 October of that year, Joseph John and Julia celebrated their Golden Wedding. The report in the newspaper for such an achievement, after outlining their lives, as detailed elsewhere, concludes as follows:

Joseph John and Julia at Parcoola

"Mrs. Pickering still does her own housework, but did not feel able to give her relatives and friends a dinner on the occasion of the golden wedding.

"Their friends around the 'Corner' felt that they could not let such an unusual occasion pass without having a social gathering. So it was arranged to give them a surprise party. So on Monday evening last, their relatives and friends gathered at their home, and everyone had a most enjoyable time. Mr. & Mrs. Pickering just knew what was going to happen in time to get cleaned up and receive their friends.

"During the evening Mr E. Atkinson spoke and congratulated Mr and Mrs Pickering upon celebrating the fiftieth anniversary of their wedding day and also upon the wonderful memory they both had, and said what a joy it was to him, to visit their home and hear them speak of their early days and experiences. At the conclusion of his remarks he presented to Mrs Pickering on behalf of her friends of the district a Morris armchair. Mr W. Loffler also spoke and presented a handsome pipe to Mr Pickering who responded for his wife and himself."

Joseph Edmund, the son who stayed at home to help his parents, married two years later at 41 years of age, a widow Myra Natt née Smith eight years his junior, and lived in a three roomed cottage near Parcoola homestead, just across the creek. Their three sons were born there and in 1939 they moved to the Geranium-Parrakie District to farm. In 1949 they sold the farm and retired to Mypolonga on the Murray River. In

Joe and Myra Pickering's old homestead at Parcoola taken in 1988

1951 they moved to Strathalbyn to care for Myra's aged mother.

Myra Julia Pickering, one of the grandchildren wrote down her memories of Parcoola:

Grandpa Pick

"In 1929, I was living with Grandma and Grandpa and went to school at Overland Corner. Grandpa Pick, as we called him, used to ride a chestnut horse called Masha. He was well over 70 years old [80 years old to be exact] then.

He used to pull the horse up to a stump that was about three feet high and then mount the horse from there. Our Dad, Douglas, did the same when he got old. He used to use the horse to bring cows in to milk. My Dad (Douglas) used to cut wood about three feet long for the boats that used to travel up and down the river and buy all their groceries off the boats. The brothers used to muster wild cattle out in the scrub and bring them home into the stable that was built with

rails cut out of the scrub.

They used to also catch wild horses called 'brumbies' and break them in then use them to work the farm.

"Grandpa Pick was a very short man, and fairly heavy-built, very happy-go-lucky

Parcoola sheds built from rails and stumps, and roofed with straw

person. Grandpa played the organ and Grandma sang. She had a lovely voice. They attended the Church of England and were very active there. They had a two roomed, underground cellar and used to separate the milk downstairs. They milked 12-15 cows in the old yard made of mallee stumps. They had a seven roomed house plus a large pantry and a lovely front garden.When all the boys were home, they used to have a lot of swaggies come in and Grandma used to feed them all. She was also Postmistress at Overland Corner Post Office. Grandpa used to kill snakes by

flicking their heads off by cracking them by the tail (like a whip).

Uncle Joe and Aunt Myra lived across the creek and had three boys, Warren, Sinclair and Joel. One day the boys were in the fowl house hitting the fowls with the door shut. Grandpa spotted them, so he sneaked down on them and shut them in the yard, took their sticks and told them they were his

Warren (9 years), Sinclair (8) and Joel (6), sons of Joe and Myra

fowls now, so he chased and hit them around the fowl house. It was a good cure."

Three months prior to Joseph John and Julia's Diamond Wedding on 31st July 1933 Samuel Daniel, the bachelor brother, died at the age of almost 78 years. Nothing much is known about him after he was left to administer his mother's estate. There are land records relating to him in the Hundred of Waterloo (therefore in the area somewhere near Port Wakefield), and he is thought to have owned a block of land at Holden Pump which he sold in 1911.

When he retired, he lived with his nephew John George, the eldest son of Joseph John, and his wife Lillie and their six children, at 52 Wattle Street, Fullarton. He paid £1.0.0d. a week board and was a great friend to the children who did not get on with their stern father.

In the meanwhile, Sarah Jane and Jeremiah had moved again, when farm lands were opened up in the Murray Mallee, to Burden, The Pines, Pompoota, Murray Bridge, until they retired. "When they shifted to the Murray the land was new and of poor quality as it is today. My father told me of the hard times of clearing the land of trees, together with poor rainfall - I think they were forced off the land." They then bought a house in Vine Street, Prospect, a suburb of Adelaide for their retirement. Sadly by this time, Jeremiah was going blind which would surely have hastened the end of their life on the farm. Memories handed down say that "Sarah was a most likeable and kind person, and was very supportive to her family," and that "the family were very close and still tended to keep in touch even though they scattered far and wide".

On 29 October 1933, at Overland Corner, Joseph John and Julia celebrated their Diamond Wedding, and although a newspaper

Joseph John and Julia's Diamond Wedding 29 October 1933

report for this has not yet been located, it would surely have been worthy of note, and an opportunity for a great celebration. Myra again recollects, "on the 60th Wedding Anniversary, they would have had over a hundred people attend. Grandpa had a lovely white beard, fairly long, and Grandma reckoned he played with his grandchildren more than his own children. Guess he had more time then, as our father, Douglas, was the same. Irma's own recollection of her grandfather, (she was only three years old when he died) "was a white bushy beard and having to kiss that."

On 5 December, 1933, shortly after these celebrations, Joseph John and Sarah Jane his sister, went before the Full Court of South

137

Joseph John ans his sister Sarah Jane Jones

Australia as defendants against John George Pickering, Lillie Adelaide Maud Pickering, Dudley Halley Pickering, Jane Goss (née Jones - Sarah's sister in law) and William Robert Rollison - Plaintiffs, consenting a Public Trustee be appointed to administer the estate of Samuel Daniel, late of Fullarton, who had died at Miss Sinclair Wood's Private Hospital, Hutt Street, Adelaide. The Plaintiffs were awarded costs of £5.19.0 and the Defendants £2.2.0d. out of the estate.

A year after Joseph John and Julia's Diamond Wedding, and shortly after his own 49th Wedding Anniversary, on 30 August 1934, Jeremiah died aged 74 years.

Letters of Administration were granted on 24 August 1934 to Carl William Lewis Mueke, and Cecil Darnton Watson, both State Chartered Accountants, as Sarah Jane and Joseph John, the natural and lawful sister and brother and the only next of kin to the deceased renounced their right and title to Letters of Administration. The estate was sworn not to exceed in value £5624.12.9d

Following the death of Jeremiah Jones, Sarah Jane very quickly followed on 24 November 1934 aged 76 years. They are buried together in the Dudley Park Cemetery, Adelaide. As Sarah Jane's property at Prospect was also transferred to Joseph John on her death, it is wondered, but not known, if the terms of the will

138

Sarah Ann, their mother, had any bearing on these rather unusual arrangements. Her estate was required to be divided equally three ways, so did Joseph John, at his mother's death, finance the other two at the time of the will, on condition that it eventually reverted to his family?

On 1 March 1937 Joseph John died - from gallstones, according to Myra - and on 28 June 1938 Julia passed away. Both were aged 87 years and are buried at Overland Corner.

In the background: the grave of Joseph and Julia; foreground: Hugo and Daisy Loffler Pickering

It is interesting to note the contents of Joseph John's will. He left all his horses and implements, with the exception of his tractor, pump and pumping plant and piping, to Joseph Edmund, the son who stayed behind to help on the farm. The rest of his real or personal estate was left in trust to pay the income to his wife, and, after her death, to Samuel Allen, a legacy of £350, to Edith, Sarah Sylvia, Julia Vida and Daisy Elfreda £150 each.

139

The balance was to be divided between Douglas Foster, Bertram Saunders, Samuel Allen and Joseph Edmund. As Julia died after Joseph, she also left a will. She left Samuel Allen the job of dividing up the whole of the household furniture and effects between her children "as he may think fit".

She then left everything else to Joseph Edmund subject to the payment of the following amounts:

Samuel Allen £350, Bertram Saunders £60, Edith, Sarah, Sylvia, Julia Vida, and Daisy Elfreda £150 each.

The following facts are given relating to Joseph John and Julia's children:

Edith married John Butler December 1895 died aged 73 years and produced 9 children;

John George married Lillie Besanko January 1905 died aged 88 years and produced 6 children;

Bertram Saunders married Kate O'Connell Nov 1901 died aged 88 years and produced 8 children;

Sarah Sylvia married Adolph Heinecke August 1910 died aged 88 years and produced 5 children;

Joseph Edmund married Myra Natt November 1925 died aged 86 years and produced 3 children;

Douglas Foster married Sophie Kuchel April 1918 died aged 74 years and produced 7 children;

Julia Vida married Bertram Fiegert September 1921 died aged 76 years and produced 5 children;

Daisy Elfreda married Hugo Loffler July 1920 died aged 73 years and produced 8 children;

Samuel Allen married Harriet Fox July 1927 died aged 52 years and produced 1 child.

It will be noted that all the children lived to a good old age, with the exception of Angus Cameron who was killed in the Great War and Samuel Allen who also served in the War - perhaps his experiences affected his health to such a degree that he died a comparatively young man.

Of Sarah Jane's family:
Robert Mitchell married Edith Burt, died aged 76 years and produced 2 children;
Jeremiah Bruce died aged 65 no issue;
Joseph Maurice married Maud Baxter died aged 81, 3 children;
Samuel Pickering married Doris Bolton, died aged 84, no issue;
Sarah Winifred died in childhood;
William Rossiter married Eileen Warnock, died aged 51, 6 children
Hartley Clifford married Ruby Wright, died aged 71, 3 children;
Elliott Allan married Bessie Champion, died aged 74, 2 children;
Jane Gertrude married Wilfred Church, died aged 63, 5 children.

The Jones family: Back row (left to right): Joseph Morris, William Rossiter, Robert Mitchell, Hartley Clifford Front row: Elliott Allan, Sarah Jane, Jane Gertrude, Samuel Pickering Jones

141

Other details are given which were collected by Irma McGregor, granddaughter of Joseph John and Julia:

When Julia Vida married in 1921 she moved to the Mannum area where her husband owned a farm. Her possessions and cow came by steamer to Pompoota where they were off loaded and collected to be taken by wagon to the farm five or six miles outback. She only had about 14 years of married life when her husband was tragically killed under a combine, while sowing grain, leaving her to bring up four young children on her own. Alan Claude Pickering, son of Bertram Saunders, lived with his Aunt Sarah Heinecke when he was four and a half years old and helped her to milk cows and get them in on horseback. Uncle Dick Heinecke made the gate locks lower down so Claude could open them to bring in the cows from the paddock. Uncle Dick taught him to swim by throwing him in the river tied with a rope. Claude crossed the river and walked several miles to school at Overland Corner for three years, then to Waikerie school until he was 14 years old. He picked apricots at 14 and then worked on Tharks Station, borrowed a bike and ride 12 miles home to Holder. He played Australian Rules Football in the Kiora team at 15. Worked as a butcher for W.H. Bruce in Waikerie. A Mr. Smith bought a horse and Claude was asked to ride it and because it bucked in the main street it cost a five dollar fine.

Then he went horse-breaking and jockeying from Mildura to Kapunda. After a race meeting in Kapunda, one weekend his boss and Claude went on to Adelaide and had their money stolen. It took them three days to walk back to Waikerie (120 miles) walking at night and sleeping during the day.

He worked at several jobs from orchard foreman at New Era (near Cadell) to pipe laying and delivery boy in horse and cart for Mum and Dad. In the 1931 flood he took over the caretaking of the ferry/

punt across the Murray River at Cadell because he could swim. Mail had to cross the river and the swollen river became rough at times with three foot high waves. He married Edna in 1933. Lived in Morgan and worked for the Council. Worked for ex-servicemen on fruit blocks at Cadell. Dorothy and Cathy were born. Paid three dollars a week and had a cow for managing two fruit blocks. Then changed jobs and worked for Mr. Jorgenson for seven dollars a week.

Took over ferry/punt for five and a half years. Cost of car, 6d. and 1d. per passenger. Used to swim the river with his kangaroo dogs - caught several rabbits with them, strapped them to the dogs and then they swam home again. Then both Edna and Claude started packing oranges at Cadell packing shed till they retired. Claude cut off two fingers sawing slats for the packing cases. Claude retired from there when he was 72 years old and lived at Waikerie.

Doug and Sophie at Moorook: the farm was a portion of Merrit property with a pug and lime room. Doug, with help from Bob Fox, rolled the scrub down with a huge gum log. To each was attached a team of horses each team controlled by a driver. They would line up a patch of scrub, race the horse team, one each side aiming the roller

Gladys and Dolla Pickering with a load of mallee stumps for the fire -no longer young children and with improved transport

143

at the timber. When the ground was sufficiently cleared, all stumps still remaining of course, a large box was fitted on the standing platform along the back of the drill. Mother would place her two small daughters, Myra and Dolla on pillows with milk bottles in the box. Four horses, under Sophie's guidance, lurched along, pulling the seed drill with one iron wheel first hitting a stump then the other wheel. The girls on occasions were tossed out.

A means of getting to school: some of the great-grandchildren of John and Sarah:Myra with Trixey, Phyllis with Ginger. Dolla with Nuttybubs and Leo with Flossy

Douglas Foster Pickering and Sophie Gertrude Kuchel, married 3 April 1918

In quick succession, the family increased in size with Phyllis, Leo, Gladys and Rae. The older children rode horseback to Moorook School. Ossie Gogel used to saddle up Myra's horse and leg her up into the saddle. For the homeward journey after school, Flossy knew where to take the right turn in the thick hop bushes to get her precious cargo home.

144

Sophie dug a large cellar, the roof and steps she made of straw and pug. As times improved, she made time to build a house. One room was 27ft by 16ft. The fireplace was large enough to hold a double bed wire mattress - not to sleep on but a place to keep milk, butter, veg, and jellies in the draught. Bacon and metwurst were hung further up the chimney. The family crushed their own grain for flour and porridge.

There never was and never will be a night to match the one when the new floor was launched. Well-wishers rolled up from every direction. At one stage, the accordionist chose to dance with his partner and play his accordion as well. Kerosene lanterns swayed in the breeze created by the white gloved men strenuously swinging their buxom partners in the Alberts, Lancers and the Polka Mazurka. There were those who really worked their way around the sawdust covered floor in pump-handle style. Others kept their elbows so arched that they resembled the handles on a flower vase. At the end of the evening, the host stood in the centre of the new floor and said, 'Thank you for coming, this floor has to be paid for so I'll just whip the hat round'.

"Doug learned to drive on a sandy farm when he bought his first car. With his family aboard for ballast, he set off over the sandy hills to the Loxton Show. He had not gone far before, looming up ahead, bogged to the axles, were seven cars. Doug pulled off the road, passed the shouting drivers, showing his driving prowess. From the other side, he then reversed and pulled each car out. The family was rewarded with free admittance to the Loxton Show."

The following information was received from Gwen Masters and Claire Webb, granddaughters to Sarah Jane Jones née Pickering:

"Jeremiah Bruce - was a stockman who never married, and lived a typical Outback life on Station properties. Gwen remembered him coming home when a child with great excitement. He stayed for a while, maybe six months, and visited the family each in turn, staying for a while with each before going bush. I think he was the black sheep of the family. He died in Queensland.

"Samuel Pickering Jones was our bachelor uncle who came to see you always with a bag of lollies and was loved by all his nephews and nieces. He eventually got married at the age of fifty. He was a Water Master and worked on an irrigation settlement and lived his married life at Tailem Bend. He never had a car, but drove a horse and cart.

"Joseph Maurice - was a farmer all his life, share farmed at Woods Point on the River Murray and eventually owned his own property of some 2,000 acres which was eventually sold and split up amongst the family. He was a hard worker with a good personality and most people enjoyed his company. He loved horses.

"Elliott Allen - worked with Joseph Maurice until he married when he bought a property in the South East and was a successful farmer. He was a Master of Hounds and a judge at the Royal Adelaide and Royal Melbourne Shows

"William Rossiter - worked on a piggery at Cungena, broke draught horses and then became a baker on Eyres Peninsular at Wudinna, and Hartley Clifford was also a baker, (his sons still carry on the business in Clare). When he and his family visited they always bought lots of cakes and goodies. He grew dahlias in the paddock adjacent to the shop and loved his one Jersey cow.

"Jane Gertrude - as the only other girl in the family (Sarah Winifred died young), Janie was the apple of her brothers' eyes. She had a passion for tennis and rowing. If you went to Adelaide you stayed with Auntie Janie. Everyone loved her. Her husband was a baker and worked for a pastry firm."

Chapter 8

When John Pickering died he left behind a wife and three children. Joseph John and Julia had eleven children and forty-seven grandchildren. Sarah Jane and Jeremiah Jones had nine children and twenty-one grandchildren. Samuel Daniel remained a bachelor with no known descendants.

What a legacy!*

In John Pickering's own words: "I am astonished when I look round me and see what I have done in so short a time, landing in this colony with 1/8d. in my pocket - it is the Lord's doings and it is marvellous in our eyes."

As for the author, perseverance won the day in the end, because if notice had been taken of the information first received, the wonderful cascade of information later obtained would still be hiding in dusty documents, and at the back of the minds of the family, perhaps never to surface.

*People with the following surnames may perhaps claim blood connection with John Pickering: Adams, Amos, Bathjen, Bell Berry, Bidell, Black, Black, Borg, Bottrell, Bowman, Bowring, Buller, Butler, Charity, Church, Clasholm, Coles, Cowland, Cranwell, Dodd, Dohnt, Dwyer, Dyer, Egan, Fiegert, Giles, Gowling, Gropler, Harvey, Hazelwood, Hein, Heinicke/Heinecke, Hill, Hoad, Honeyman, Hook, Hughes, Hunter, Jones, Kipping, Kuchel, Lahne, Leckie, Loffler, Lokan, Lombardi, Markow, McCullough/Cullock, McDonald, McFarlane, McGregor, McNamara, Meznar, Mills, Mitchel, Mohylenko, Murphy, Murrie, Nettle, Pabot, Perry, Platten, Pope, Roenfeld, Rossack, Rowley, Saviour, Smelt, Smith, Steer, Stockyard, Stone, Suroser, Trezise, Villis, Wareham, Webb, Weckert, Wellins, Wilkinson, Willshire, Wilson, Woolford, Worrall, Wynn, Yates.

Afterword

The author has not as yet been able to visit Australia. The inspiration to write this story was the discovery of letters sent home by John Pickering about his new life in a new country. If he had not been capable of putting pen to paper, his story and that of his descendants would never have been told.

With nothing more than the framework of these letters on which to base my research, I have been able, with a lot of help from his descendants, to bring the story to the beginning of the twenty-first century and introduce cousin to cousin. My research has been entirely dependent on the generous help and good will of the extended family which enabled me to construct the family trees. The personal memories are a particular treasure, and without Irma McGregor's hard work, it would have been impossible to bring the story forward to the present.

Because I was working from such a huge distance, local information would have been very limited, if not non-existent, without the very generous and unstinting help of Mrs E. A. Bellman, who allowed me to use large extracts from her publication History of Steelton District and James and Marilyn Potter, local historians, of Salisbury, who did voluntary research in the Salisbury area. I am also indebted to Dr Arnold Hunt for research into the Primitive Methodist Church and the life of the Rev. John Gibbon Wright.

Professional help came from Andrew Peake and, in the early days, the South Australia Genealogy and Heraldry Society Inc. The

Soldier Career Management Agency in Melbourne very generously supplied the details of the military career of Angus Cameron Pickering.

My contribution has been to attempt to link all this random research in order to make a coherent account of a family's expanding life in a new country. There are many gaps and many questions, and I leave it to the present family and anyone else with a curious mind to attempt to complete the story.

For example: Did Joseph Bass Miller sail on the same ship as John Pickering?

Is there really no memorial of any kind to John Pickering? Surely Sarah Ann would have made some provision for a recognition of his life? Was there no set of books provided for the Pancharpoo school, no pew or bench for the chapel, no font ?

Does Joseph John's farmer's day-book still exist?

Is there, somewhere, a photograph of Samuel Daniel, a very shadowy figure in adulthood?

Who was Angus Cameron? How did it come about that this clerk formed a business partnership with an already successful farmer?

Answers to these and many other questions would be gratefully received by the author.

The original letters which had been written phonetically and without punctuation have been transcribed and silently punctuated for ease of reading. The spelling of the names in the family tree are as provided by members of the families concerned

Original manuscripts of the full research have been deposited in the

Staffordshire County Record Office in Stafford, England, the Mitchell Library, Sydney, NSW, and the Mortlock Library, Adelaide, South Australia.

Angus Cameron Pickering's grave in Outtersteene Cemetery, near Bailleul, was visited by the author in the mid 1990s and copies of his mother's letters were placed inside the visitors' book in the hall of remembrance.

Acknowledgements

Geoff Braine and Barbara Lanham for extracts from the diary of the 151-day voyage of the 'Africana' in 1865;

Mrs A.E.Bellman for her kind permission to use parts of her *History of Steelton District* and who also published the helpful *History of Saddleworth*;

James Potter, ex-President of the Salisbury Local History Society for his help with Salisbury's early history;

Australian Imperial Force for copies of the letters referring to the death of Angus Cameron Pickering.

Bibliography

The Cornish Miner in Australia or Cousin Jack Down Under - Phillip J. Payton (Dyllansow Truran);
The Cornish Farmer in Australia - Phillip J. Payton (Dyllansow Truran);
I called it Salisbury - A.P.Harvey (Salisbury & District Historical Society);

Little Para Pilgrims - James L. Potter (Salisbury & District Historical Society);
Salisbury South Australia, A History of Town and District - John H. Lewis (Investigator Press);
Saddleworth, Hub of the Wheel - Elinor A. Bellman (Saddleworth Progress Association);
Tracing your Family History in Australia - Nick Vine Hall (Rigby).

New House, North Lake, Doug and Sophie's home built in the 1930s. Sophie made all the concrete bricks.

Leo Pickering with his pet kangaroo

153

Riverland A Grade Champion Basketball team in the late 1940s
(l. to r.) Rae Pickering, Kath Feeder, Jan Spiller, Nancy McFarlane,
Dolla Pickering, Meg Sutton, Glady Pickering

Bertram and Kate Pickering and family

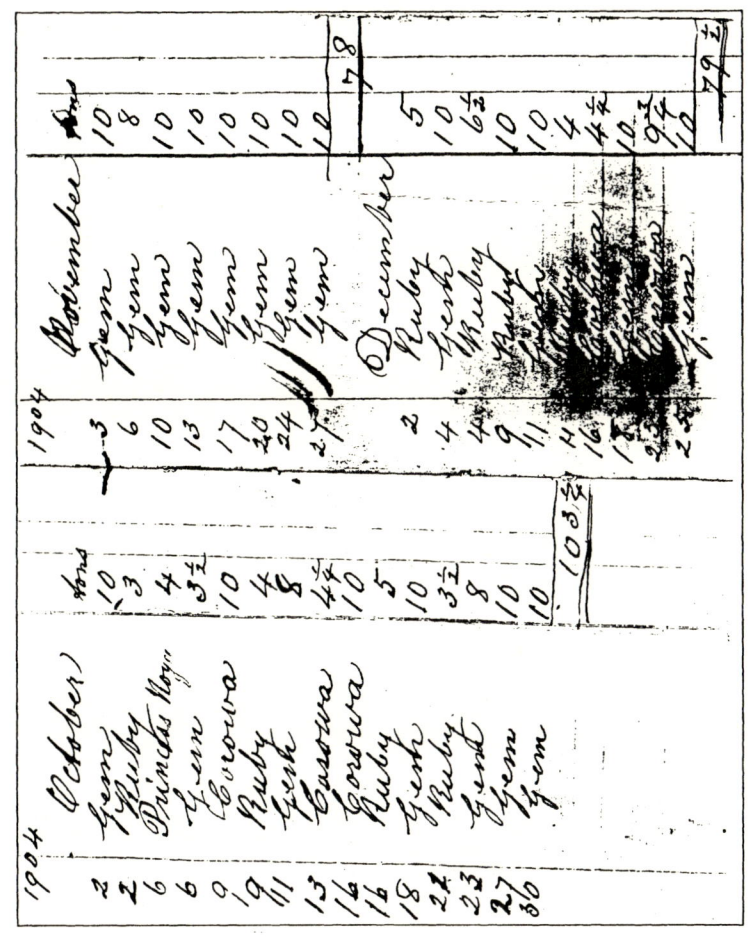

Two pages from the Day-book of 1904 when Joseph John and Julia
were at Overland Corner

155

The Diamond Wedding of Bertram and Kate Pickering in 1961
Back row: Claude, Ron, Alex, Jean, Joe. Front row: Bert, Kate, Bertram, Clem.
The youngest, Irene, is absent from the photograph

Eileen Winter's 70th Birthday Party 25 August 1991
Back row: Val Masters, Joan Jones, Brian Jones, Glen Pitman, Colin Winter, Murray
Church, Bruce Pitman. Front row: Claire Webb, Gwen Masters, Marion Pitman,
Eileen Winter, Rosalie Church, Alison Pitman

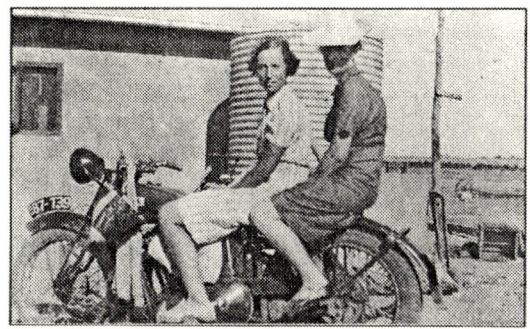

Glady and Dolla at the back of the house at Lake Bonney (North Lake)

Dolla May Pickering with
baby Irma Rio Pickering
sitting out the back of
Parcoola about 1935

Murray cod - early fishing in the River Murray. Douglas always said that fish would bite on a red rag on a hook when they first went to live at Parcoola

Doug or Leo Pickering with the Fargo lorry and a load of cocky chaff in 1933

Rita Dodd, Freda (Doll) Stone née Pickering and Geoff Stone, Edith Butler, Edric Dodd, John Butler

Dipping buckets of grapes before hanging them to dry on racks. In the background is the McFarlane property

Trays of apricots cut by Myra and gang at Kingston on Murray 1933

River Murray near Parcoola. Phyllis and Dolla Pickering, Gordon Clasohm and
Angus Heinecke

Clement Pickering, son of Bertram and
Catherine, aged 2 years - 1918

Julia Pickering aged 80 with her
great granddaughter Lavina Butler
aged 8 months - April 1931

Grace, Rita, Dolly and Effie Butler

Family Legend and a Sideboard

as written by Mrs Sarah Heinicke, grand-daughter of John Pickering

"John Pickering came out from England to South Australia as he thought to make a fortune in a few years. He paid his fare out here. He took up land on the River Light. He left his one little boy and wife in England, her mother and her kept a small shop. When he was settled he sent her enough money to pay her fare to come out here, when she heard a boat was leaving for South Australia. So she packed her cases and went down to have a look over the boat, but the conditions were so rough, she said to the captain, 'I could never live under such conditions, nothing convenient,' so she went back to her mother. Again her husband sent her enough money to pay her fare out here, so she packed her cases and went to have another look. The captain took her around the boat, but again she said, 'I could not live under such conditions.' As it was getting very late in the evening the captain persuaded her to sleep on the boat and go back in the morning. But the wind got up during the night, and when she awoke she was miles out to sea, and her boy was five years old when she arrived here at Adelaide in 1854.

John Pickering had a clerk with him named Angus Cameron, and they built a boat and put a sail up. Toward evening they went out to give it a trial on the River Light. His wife said to him, 'I'm sure there is a storm coming up' and it did. There was wind, lightning, and thunder, and it was pouring with rain. She waited up all night and when daylight came the River Light was in flood. They found nothing of the two men and the boat.

She then sold the farm and thirteen months after she married the Rev. John Tallack, a Methodist Minister at Strathalbyn and she educated her three children, Joseph, Samuel and Sarah.

After a few years John Tallack has to give up preaching as it

162

affected his throat. Mrs Tallack had a farm near Auburn so Joseph and Samuel went farming and John Tallack built a room on the

house and he was handy with tools and he made this sideboard and gave it to my Mum and Dad for a wedding present on October 22nd 1873 at Auburn."

Long after completing my original manuscript, I received this 'handed-down' version of the family history, dug up from a branch of the National Trust in South Australia. It is fascinating to see how accurate the framework of the story is and reinforces the theory that one should always investigate family legends.

The Corner's oldest Residents
Mrs Pickering given 82nd Birthday Party

Overland Corner May 15

 Saturday evening a number of local residents tendered a birthday party to Mrs Joseph Pickering senior, at her home 'Parcoola', the occasion being her82nd birthday. Mr and Mrs Pickering are the oldest residents of the Overland Corner district having arrived there from Yacka over 35 years ago.
 Mrs Pickering, who carries her years lightly is still bright and has a ready wit. She is loved throughout the district for her kindly nature. Mr Pickering, who is also hale and hearty is two years his wife's senior. The party took the form of a dance, several novelty items being introduced. Mr Arthur Robertson, in a few well chosen words, wished Mrs Pickering 'many happy returns of the day' on behalf of those present. Mr Pickering responded for his wife, and Mrs Pickering then cut the Birthday cake, decorated with 82 candles, which was made and presented by her daughter Mrs Heinicke. A lucky spot waltz was won by Mrs S. Pickering and Mr A. Heinicke, the Monte Carlo by Miss T. Loffler and Mr A. Heinicke, and a streamer dance by Miss Jean Smith and Mr G. Boxall.

Quoted in *Waikerie - Gateway to the Riverland* by J. Nunn 1991

Not in the Australian outback but in the middle of England. Far left is Joseph Pickerill, younger brother by ten years of John Pickering of South Australia, and the place is Beacroft Farm, Stafford Road, Cannock, in Staffordshire. The land on which the farm stood is now the site of many of Cannock's public buildings - the hospital, the High School, Council Offices, shopping centre and 'bus station.

The photograph , which featured in the *Cannock Advertiser,* also shows Joseph's two sons: George, second left, the father-in-law I never knew, and John, extreme right. Mr W. J. Wood, in overalls, was the owner of the 'first portable machine ever used in the district to shear sheep,' and the remaining person is Mr S. Bickford.

Joseph was referred to in John's letters as having 'stood in his own light' when urged to emigrate, and advised 'to do the best he can now he is wed.' In fact he was just as successful, or even more so, than his brother.

He married Harriet Parker, ten years his senior, in 1855, and they had one son, Charles. Harriet died in 1874 and Joseph married Martha Emery, fifteen years his junior. They had nine children.

He farmed at Beacroft from about 1886 to 1916 and during this time was known throughout the County as 'the father of local farming.' His keen business abilities and agricultural knowledge led to his being elected to the Cannock Urban Council and the Cannock School Board, and at the time of his death in 1917, he was a Manager of the Cannock National Schools and a member of Wood's Charity. He was also a stalwart member of St Luke's Church, Cannock.

A family gathering in Cannock, England, in the early 1900s. The occasion was the wedding of Joseph Pickerill's eldest daughter Hannah to Harold Baker. On either side of the bride and groom are Joseph and Martha (née Emery) his second wife. Seated on the ground are their two youngest daughters, Harriet (left) who died in 1916 at the age of 27 years of appendicitis, and Ruth Helena who remained a spinster and became a school teacher. It was on her death in 1980 that the letters from John Pickering were discovered. Standing (back row), second from the left is George, my husband's father, and next to him is a cousin, Polly, then John, eldest in the second family with his wife Georgina. Then comes Charles, only child of the first marriage to Harriet Parker with his wife, Emma (née Benton. Beyond Emma is Martha Ann (Pat) twin sister to George, who like her sister remained single. At the end is Mary, who married Oscar Anslow, a widower with three children.

John and Georgina produced two daughters and one son, George and Madeline one son, Hannah and Harold one son, and Charles and Emma four sons and two daughters - a total of eleven grandchildren, which compares poorly with the South Australian total.

Today there are very few retaining the Pickerill name.

Family Trees

Sincere thanks are due to all who have provided me with details which have enabled me to provide the following family trees. The compilation of such charts is fraught with danger: information is not always accurate or even forthcoming. Please forgive, therefore, any errors, especially where I have had to give two spellings (e.g. Heinecke, Heinicke; Mitchel, Mitchell). It will perhaps help you to forgive me if you remember that the subject of our book was variously called Pickrel, Pickerel, Pickerill. Piggeren and Pickering.

FAMILY TREE 1 The children and grandchildren of John and Sarah Pickering

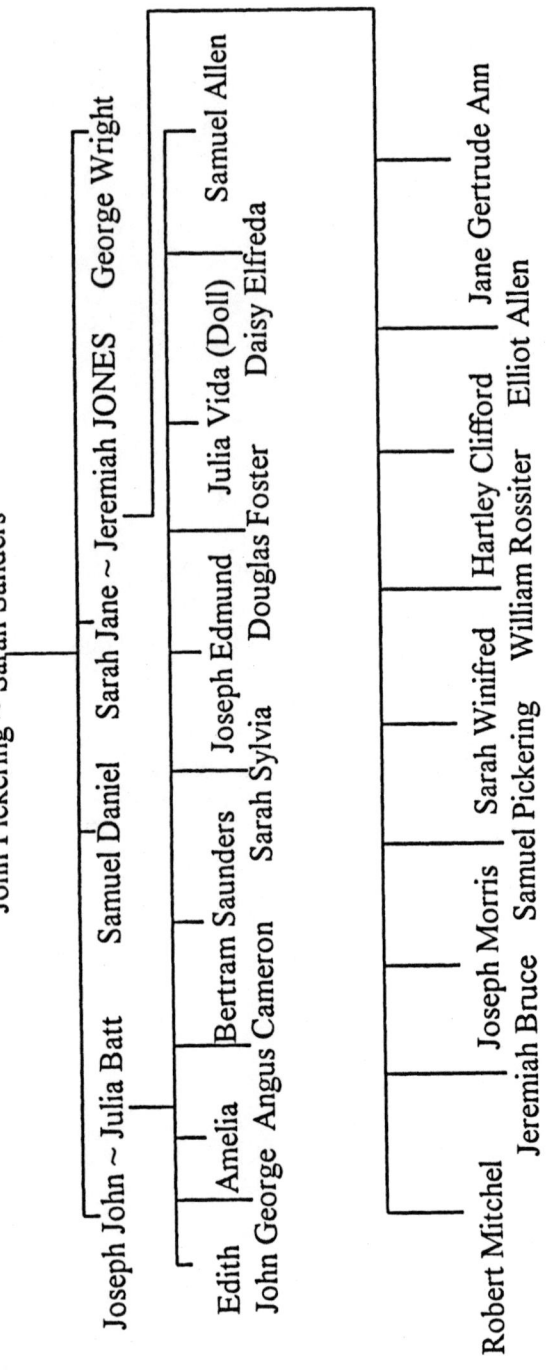

Samuel Allen married Harriet Fox and they had a son Neil.
Other descendants figure in the following family trees. E & O E

FAMILY TREE 2 The children of Joseph John and Julia Pickering and their spouses

Joseph John Pickering ~ Julia Batt

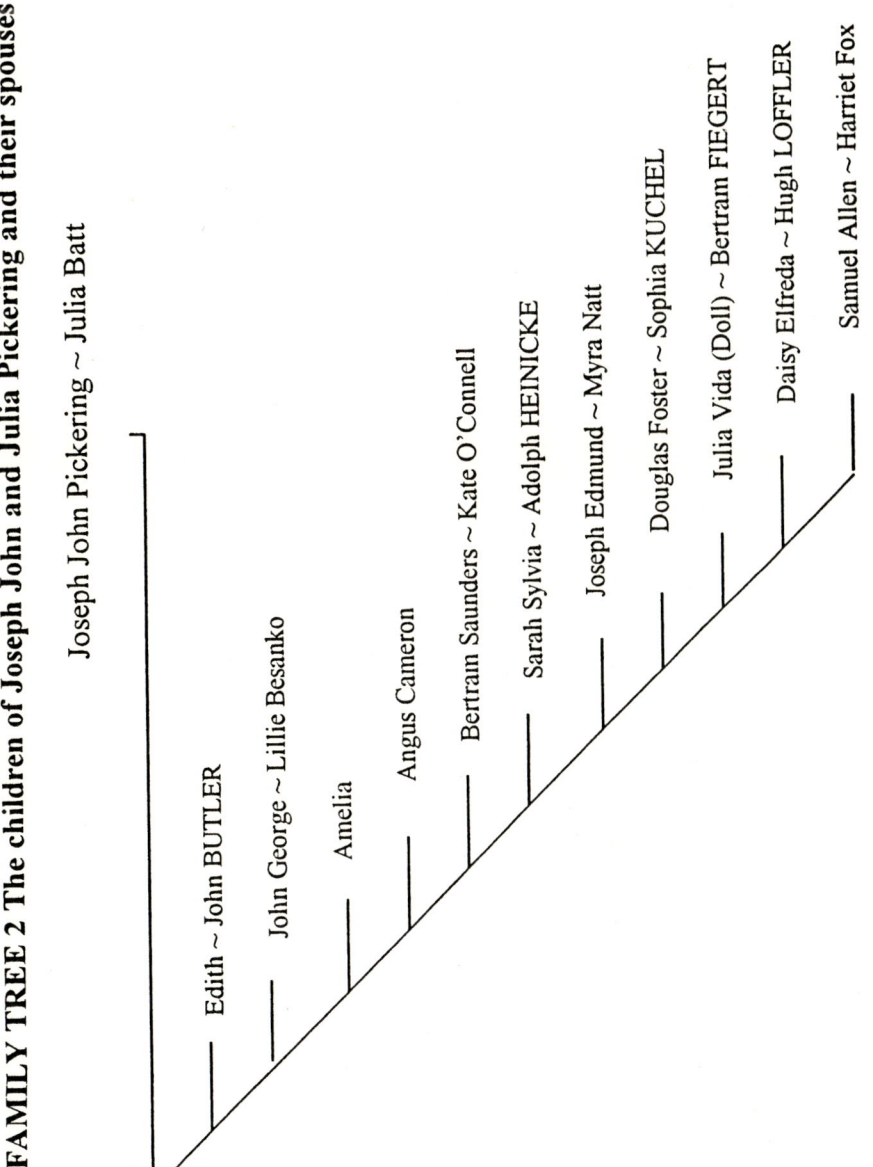

Edith ~ John BUTLER

John George ~ Lillie Besanko

Amelia

Angus Cameron

Bertram Saunders ~ Kate O'Connell

Sarah Sylvia ~ Adolph HEINICKE

Joseph Edmund ~ Myra Natt

Douglas Foster ~ Sophia KUCHEL

Julia Vida (Doll) ~ Bertram FIEGERT

Daisy Elfreda ~ Hugh LOFFLER

Samuel Allen ~ Harriet Fox

FAMILY TREE 3 The children and grandchildren of Sarah Jane and Jeremiah Jones

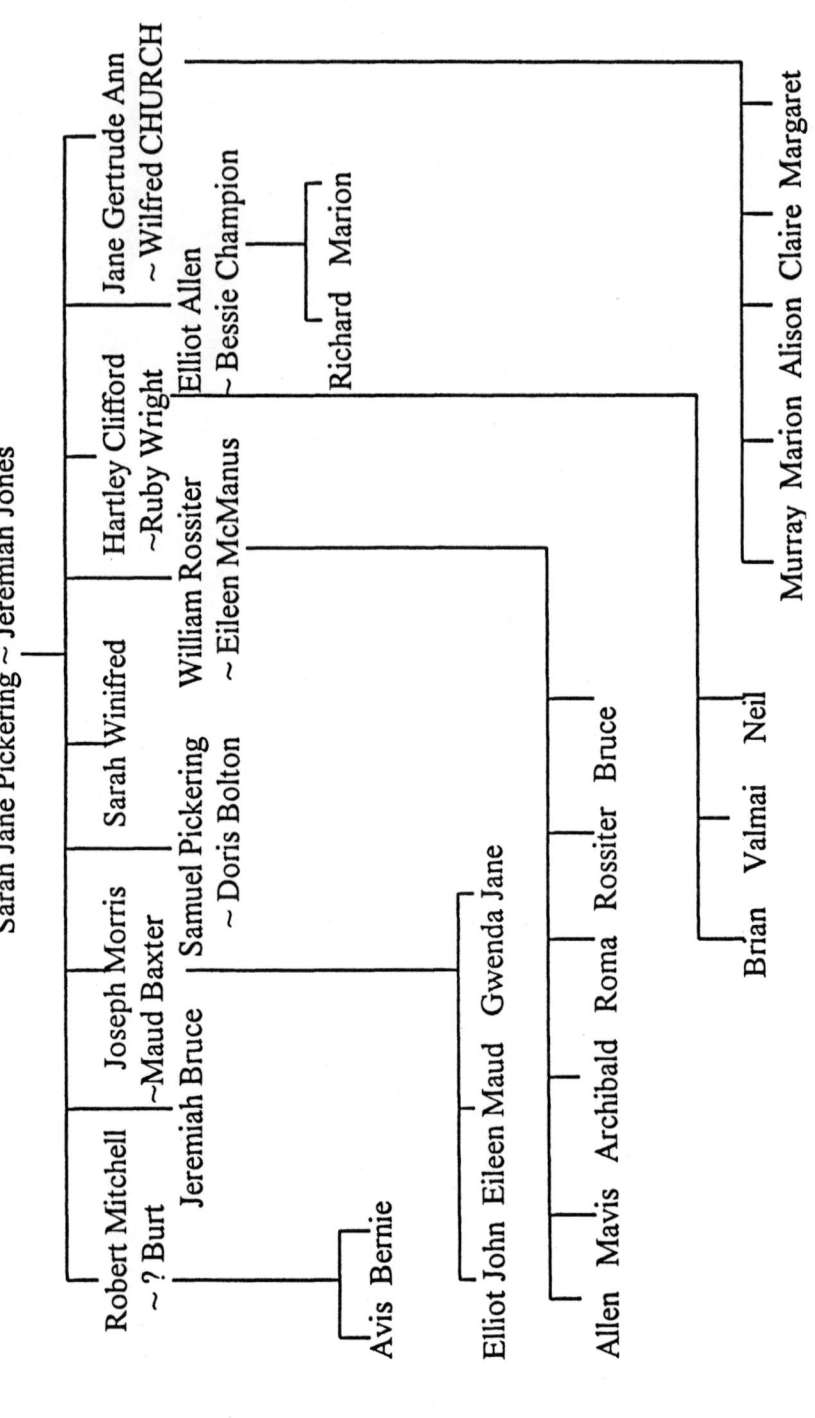

FAMILY TREE 4 The progeny of Edith Julia and John Stewart Butler

Edith Julia Pickering ~ John Stewart Butler

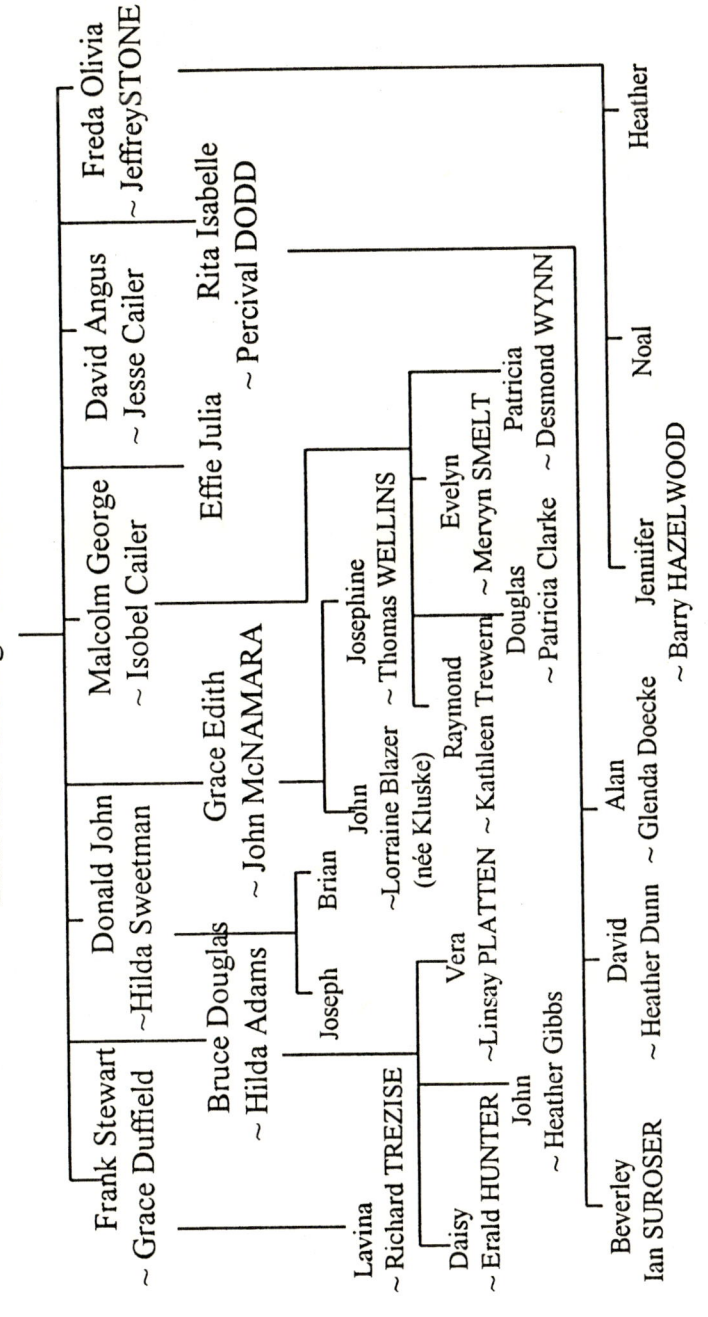

FAMILY TREE 4a Edith Julia Pickering and John Stewart Butler (continued)

Lavina
~Richard TREZISE

Daisy
~Erald HUNTER

Sharon Cathy Christine Keith

Carolyn Gayle Brenton

John
~Heather Gibbs

Helen Janice Angela Russel Vanessa Tanya
~Neil HARVEY
Kylie Tyson

Vera
~Linsay PLATTEN

John~Lorraine Blazer Josephine
~Thomas WELLINS

Andrew Daniel Timothy(twins)Katrina

Raymond Douglas Evelyn
~Kathleen Trewern ~Patricia Clarke ~Mervyn SMELT

Lynette Neil

Christine Murray Trevor

Patricia
~Desmond WYNN Beverley David Alan
~Ian SUROSER ~Heather ~Glenda
Dunn Doecke

Sandra Teena Mark

Michael Maryanne Anthony Paul

Malcolm Robert Sharon
~Greg HONEYMAN ~John STOCKFORD

Eileen

Nicolle

Wendy Dawn David

Jay Douglas

Jennifer~Barry Hazelwood

Graham Velice Tasmin

Margaret Alan John Helen Gregory Catherine Anthony Timothy

Graham
~Daphne Schultz

Marie Craig Simon

Ian
~Pamela Neale

Christine

Peter
/Beverley Grenfell

Teresa Ann

David
/Judith Shovan

Tammy

Kelvin
/Carleen Vogt

Cindy Michael

Dianne

FAMILY TREE 5 The progeny of John George and Lillie Besanko

John George Pickering ~ Lillian Besanko

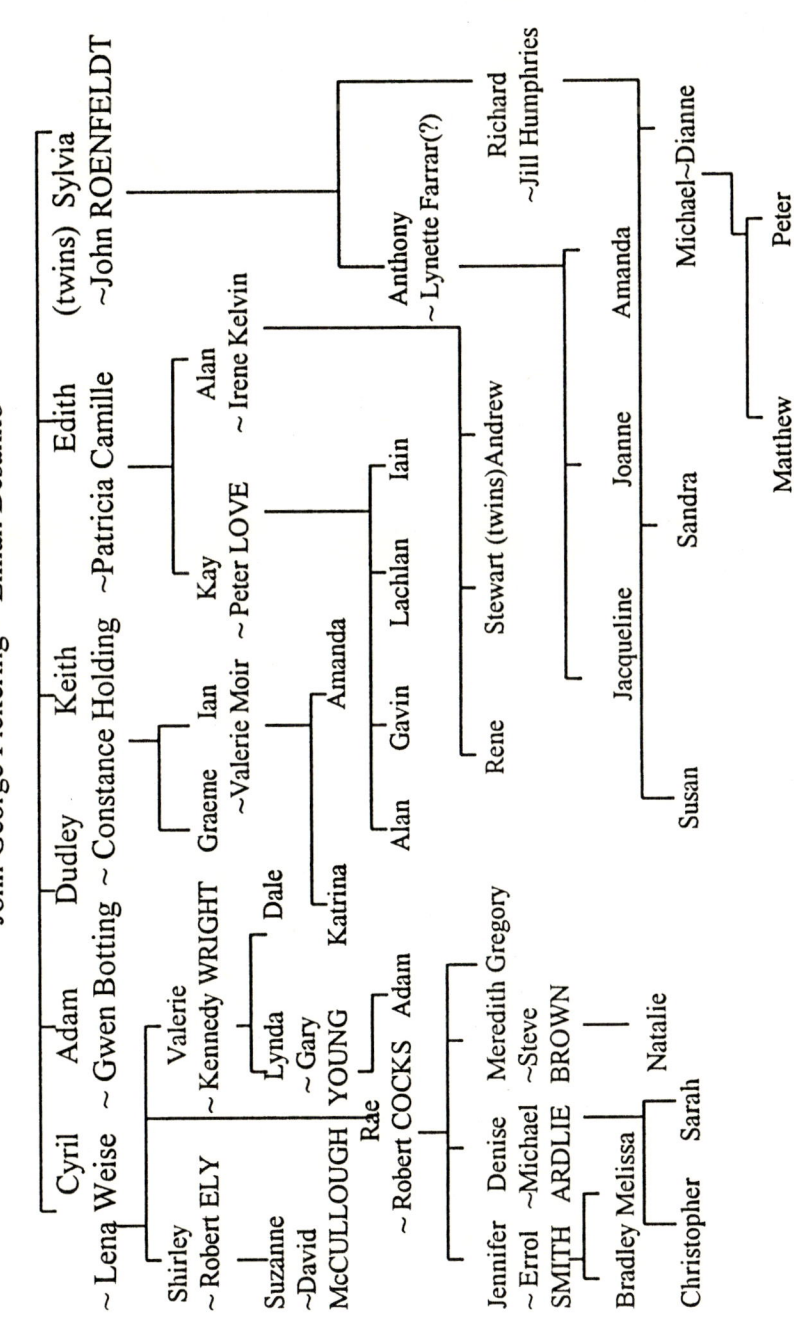

FAMILY TREE   The family of Bertram Saunders Pickering and Catherine O'Connell

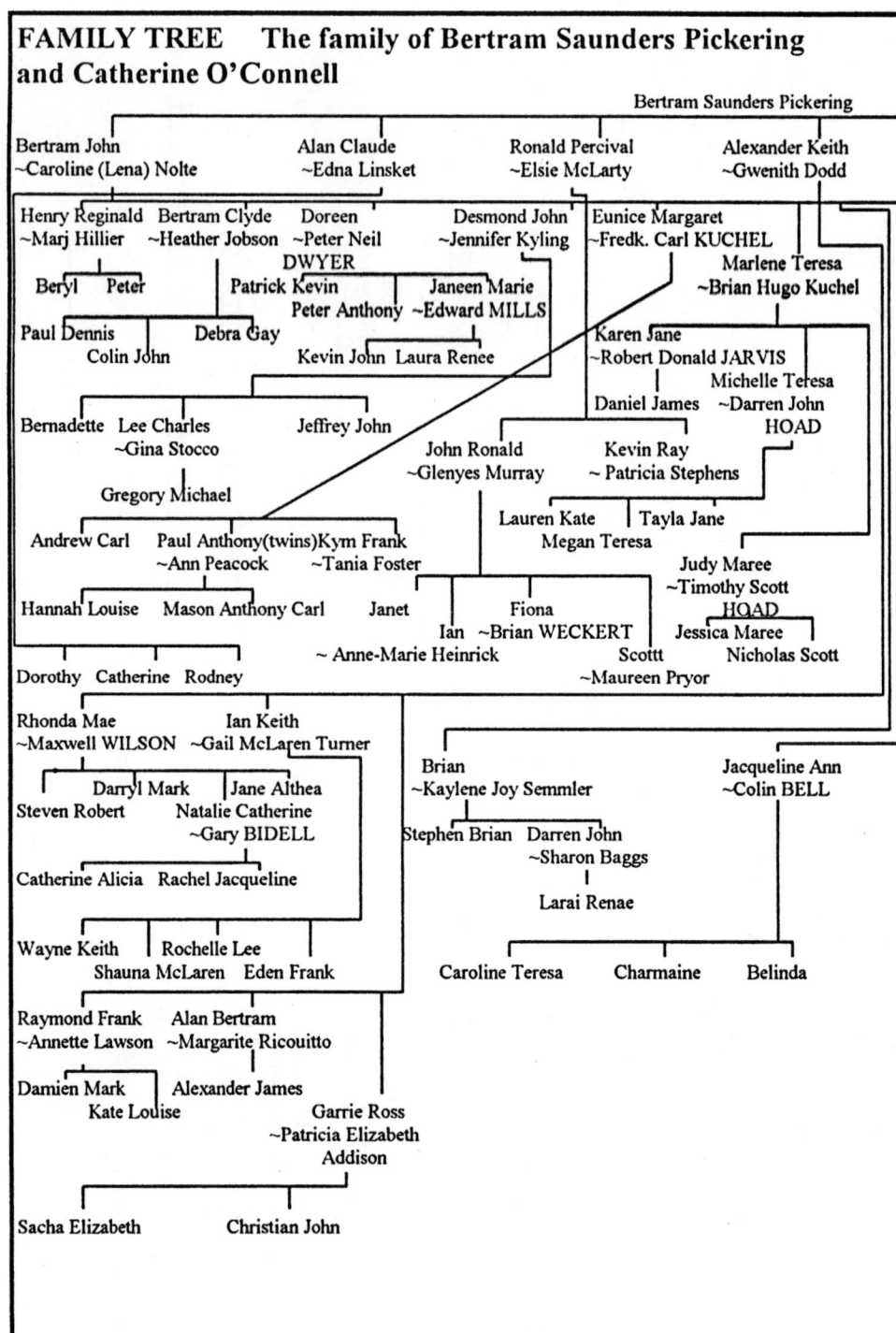

~ Catherine O'Connell

Ivy Jean
~Mervyn Roy
ROWLEY

Joseph Clyde
~Florence Ann
O'Calligan

Clement Danielle
~Joyce Anzac
Pinches

Dorothy Irene
~Alick Russell
STEER

Colette Jean
~Ronald KIPPING

Marilyn Ann
~ Peter MURRIE

Wendy Irene
~(1)Berend de VRIES
~(2)Rodney CRANWELL

Paul   Miranda

Darren Peter   Stephen Brent

Jannifer
~Michael BERRY

Gregory Neil
/Tania Widdison

Christopher Mark
~Kate Hogan

James

Christopher Michael
~Heather Keen

Wendy Ann

David Andrew
~Tracey Stevens

Robyn Ann
~Colin Thomas MITCHELL

Jessica   Mitchell   Maggie

Kylie Ann   Natasha Louise

Graham Clyde
~Louise Fresillo

Joan Patricia
~(1)Peter WORRAL
~(2) ? LOMBARDI

Helen
~Geoff LOKAN

Darren Andrew
~Sally Gaudzinskas

Tracy (W)   Sonny (L)

Tiana Louise

Jacqueline (W)
~Andrew TINKER-CASSON

Sharon Louise
~Cary HOWELL   Madison

Bianca Louise   Jarod John

Danielle   Melissa   Krista   Faye   Andrew   Ashley Malcolm
                                     ~Malcolm
                                     GOWLING

Travis Malcolm   Luke Adam
          Tabra   Jessica Louise

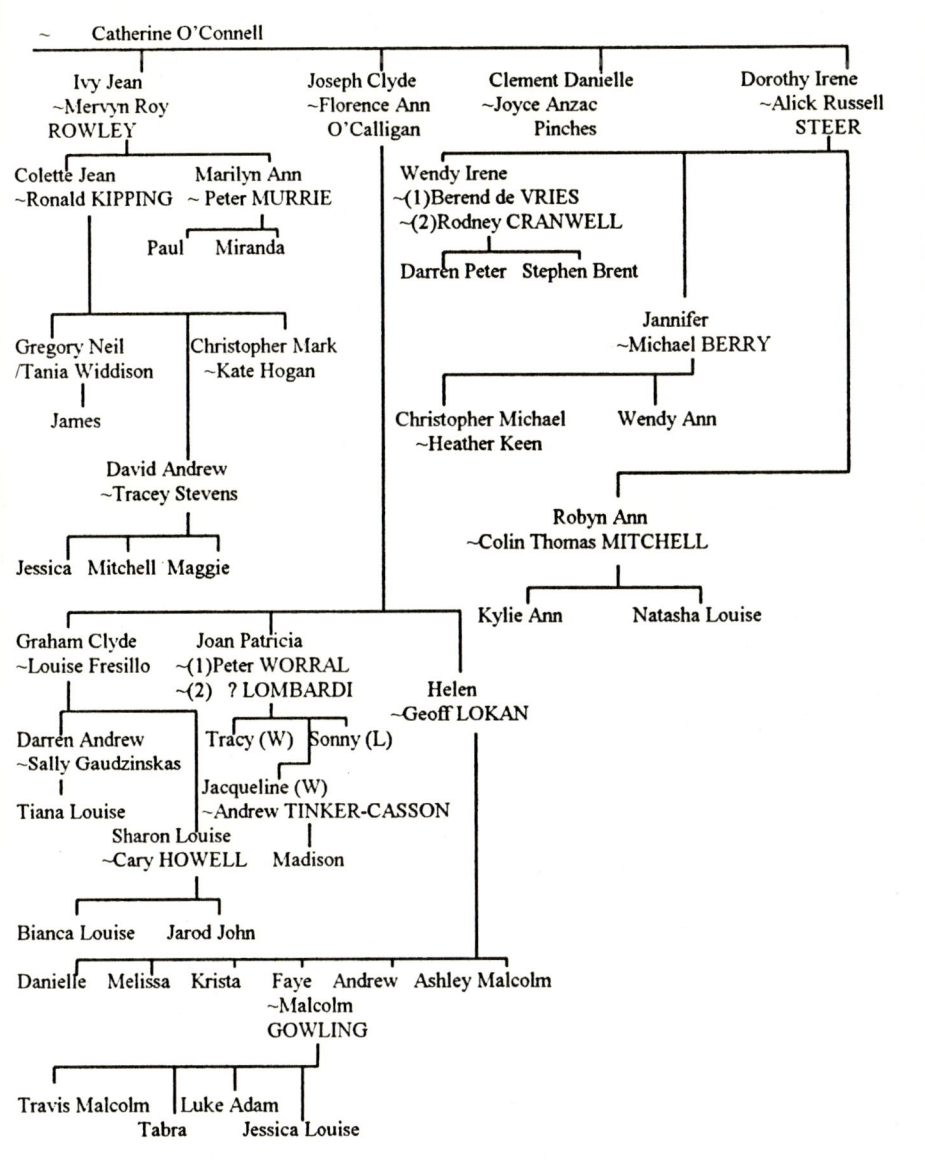

FAMILY TREE 7 Joseph Edmund Pickering and Myra Anne Smith

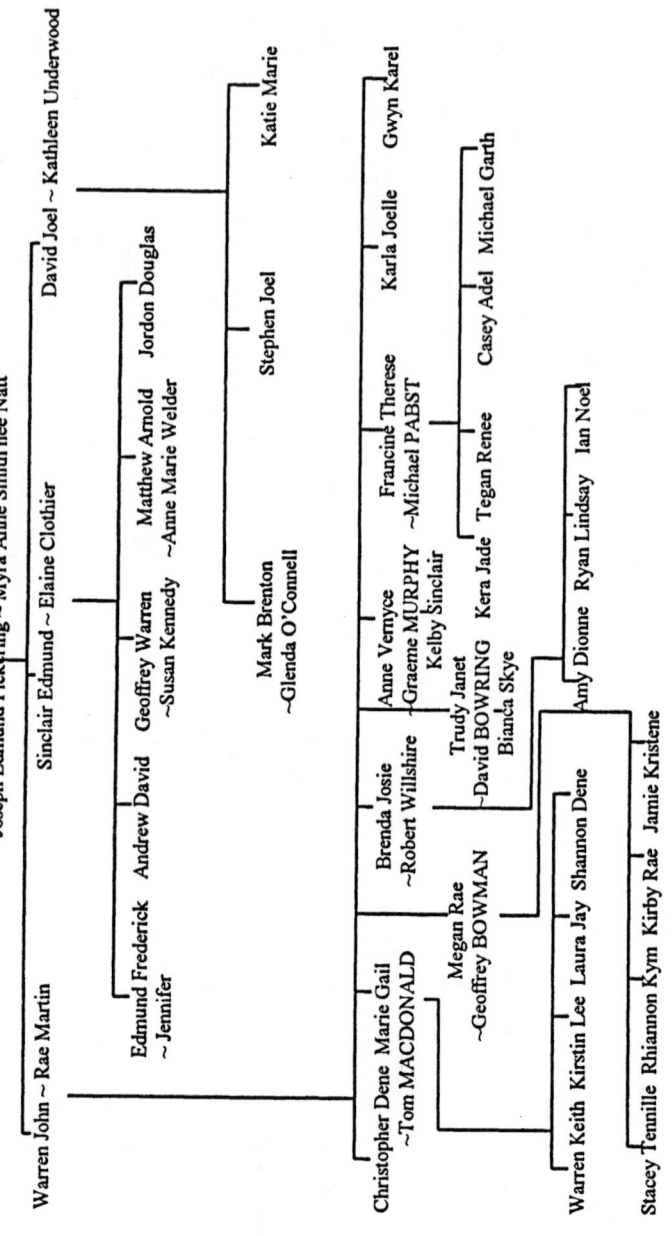

Joseph Edmund Pickering ~ Myra Anne Smith née Natt

Warren John ~ Rae Martin

Sinclair Edmund ~ Elaine Clothier

David Joel ~ Kathleen Underwood

Edmund Frederick ~ Jennifer

Andrew David

Geoffrey Warren ~ Susan Kennedy

Matthew Arnold ~ Anne Marie Welder

Jordon Douglas

Mark Brenton ~ Glenda O'Connell

Stephen Joel

Katie Marie

Christopher Dene

Marie Gail ~ Tom MACDONALD

Megan Rae ~ Geoffrey BOWMAN

Brenda Josie ~ Robert Willshire

Anne Vernyce ~ Graeme MURPHY / Kelby Sinclair

Trudy Janet ~ David BOWRING / Bianca Skye

Francine Therese ~ Michael PABST

Karla Joelle

Gwyn Karel

Kera Jade

Tegan Renee

Casey Adel

Michael Garth

Amy Dionne

Ryan Lindsay

Ian Noel

Warren Keith

Kirstin Lee

Laura Jay

Shannon Dene

Stacey Tennille

Rhiannon Kym

Kirby Rae

Jamie Kristene

FAMILY TREE 8 Daisy Elfreda and Hugo Alfred Loffler

Daisy Elfreda~Hugo Alfred Loffler

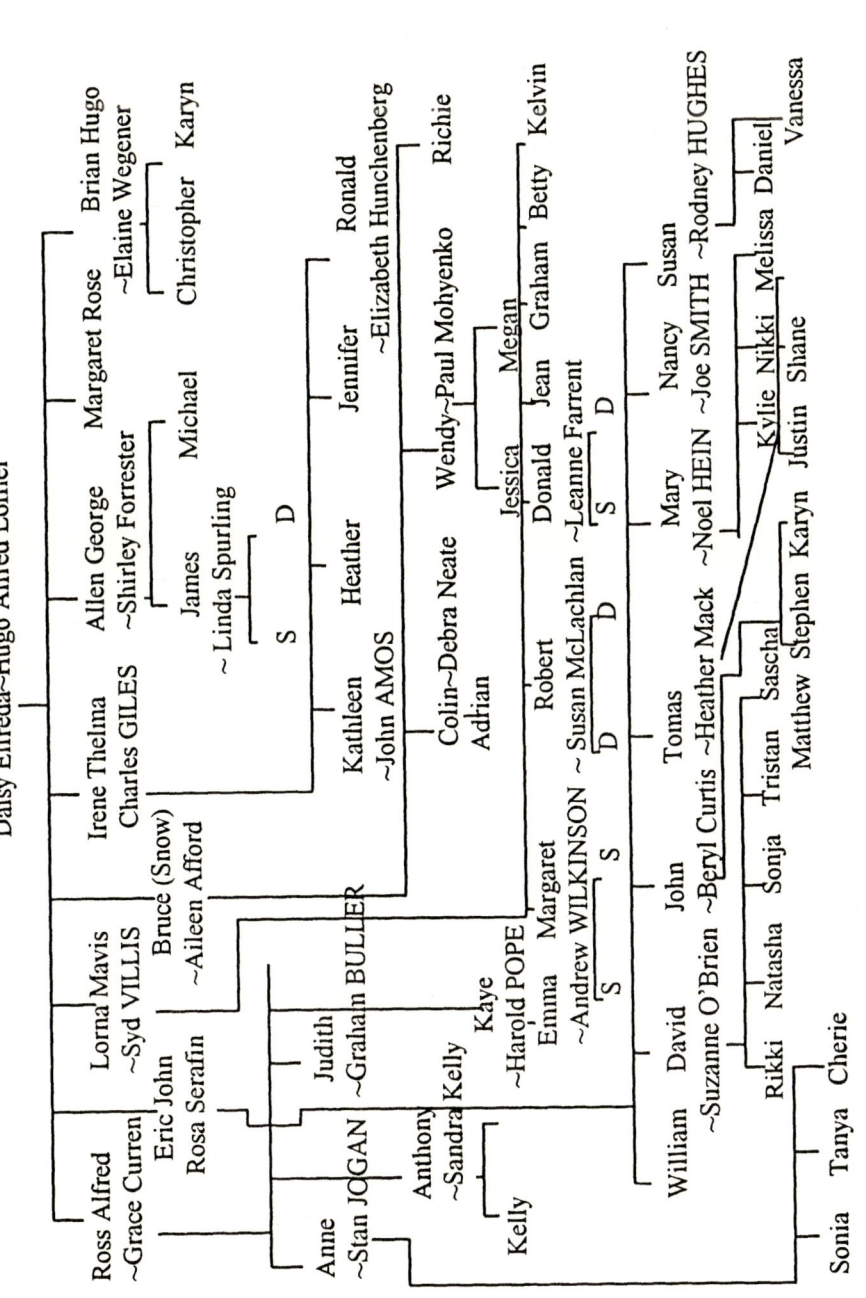

FAMILY TREE 9 Douglas Foster and Sophia Gertrude Kuchel

Douglas Foster~Sophia Gertrude Kuchel

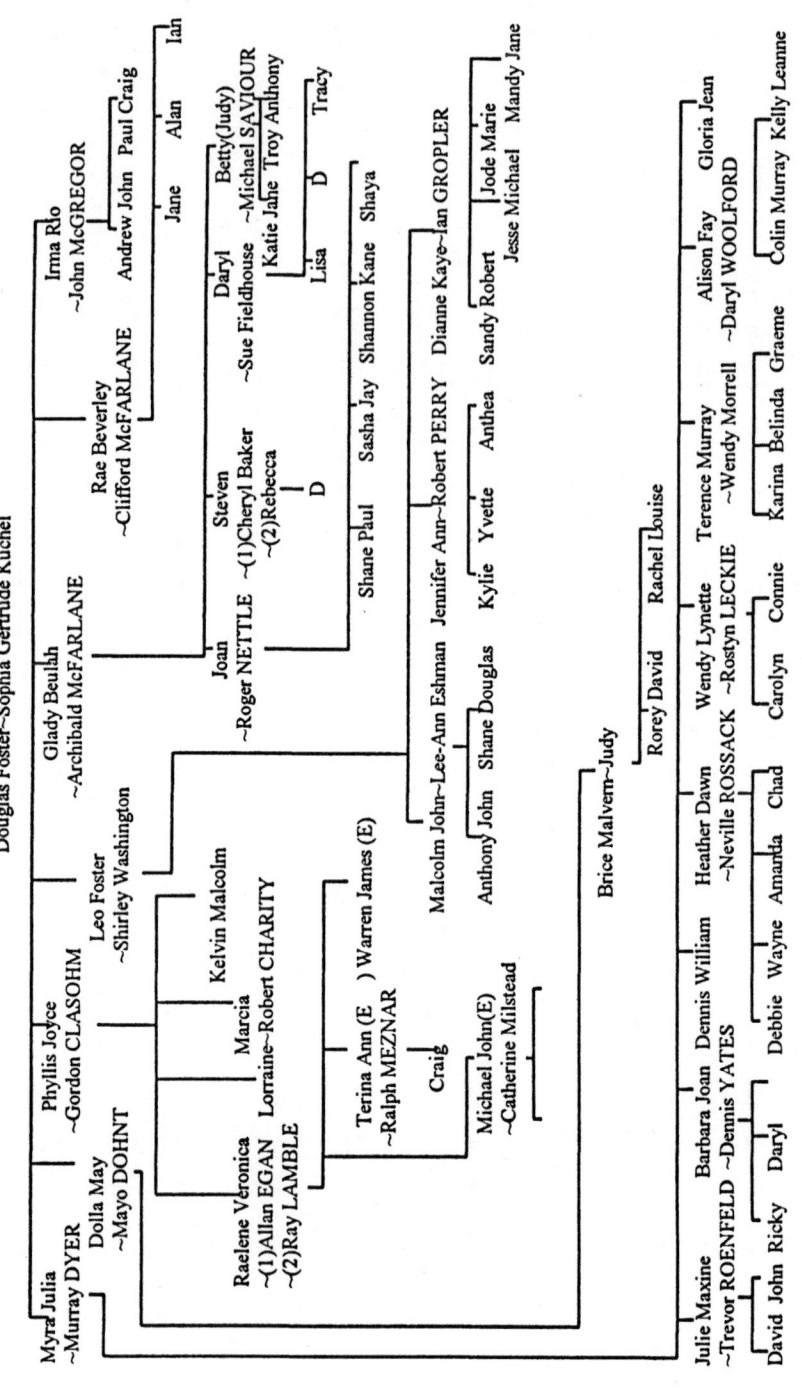

FAMILY TREE 10 Julia Vida and Berthold Heinrich Fiegert

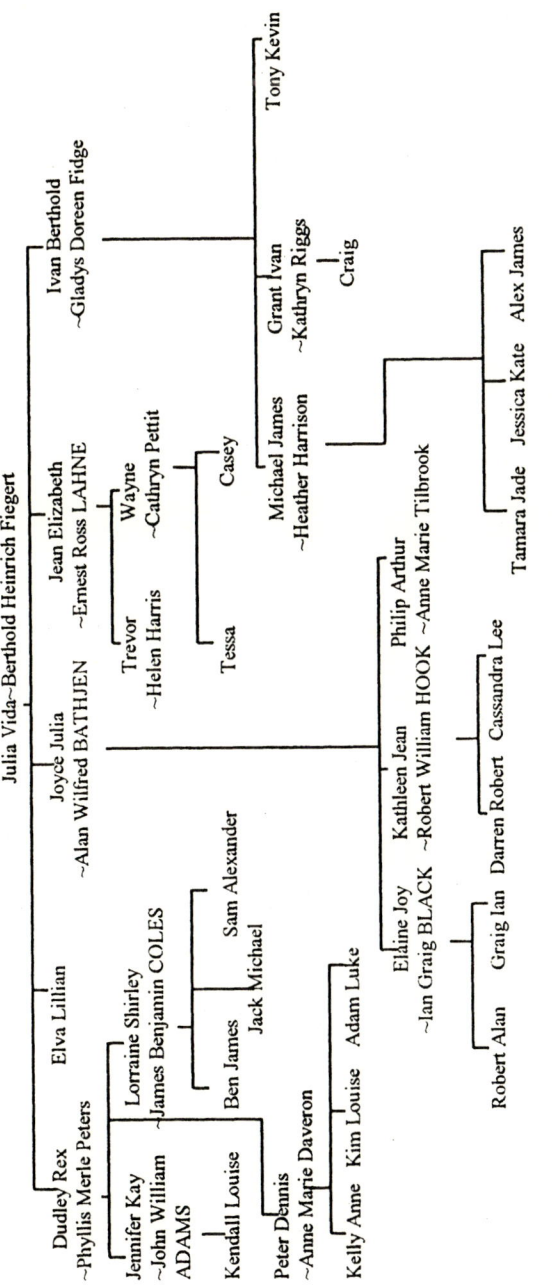

Julia Vida~Berthold Heinrich Fiegert

Dudley Rex
~Phyllis Merle Peters

Elva Lillian

Joyce Julia
~Alan Wilfred BATHJEN

Jean Elizabeth
~Ernest Ross LAHNE

Ivan Berthold
~Gladys Doreen Fidge

Jennifer Kay
~John William
ADAMS

Lorraine Shirley
~James Benjamin COLES

Trevor
~Helen Harris

Wayne
~Cathryn Pettit

Grant Ivan
~Kathryn Riggs

Tony Kevin

Kendall Louise

Ben James   Sam Alexander

Jack Michael

Tessa

Casey

Michael James
~Heather Harrison

Craig

Peter Dennis
~Anne Marie Daveron

Kelly Anne Kim Louise Adam Luke

Elaine Joy
~Ian Graig BLACK

Kathleen Jean
~Robert William HOOK

Philip Arthur
~Anne Marie Tilbrook

Robert Alan

Graig Ian Darren Robert Cassandra Lee

Tamara Jade Jessica Kate Alex James

FAMILY TREE 11 Sarah Sylvia and Gustav Adolf Heinicke

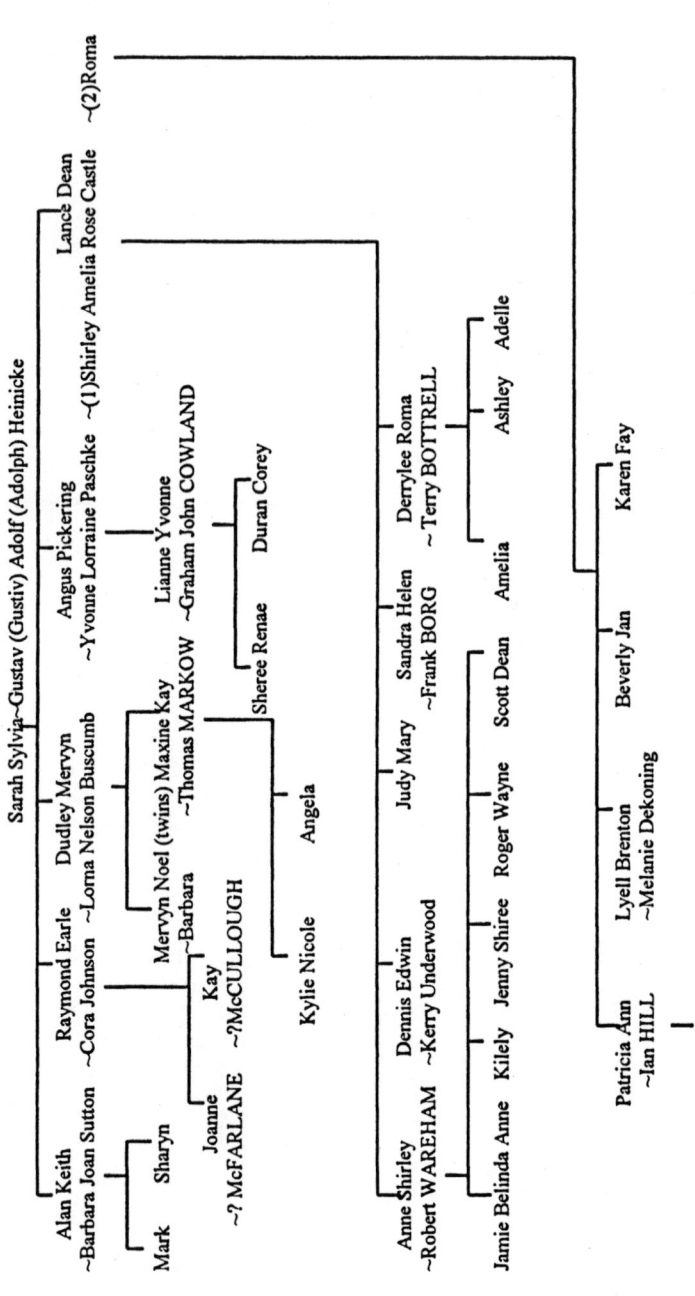

Sarah Sylvia~Gustav (Gustiv) Adolf (Adolph) Heinicke

Raymond Earle
~Cora Johnson

Dudley Mervyn
~Loma Nelson Buscumb

Angus Pickering
~Yvonne Lorraine Paschke

Lance Dean

~(1)Shirley Amelia Rose Castle   ~(2)Roma

Alan Keith
~Barbara Joan Sutton

Mark   Sharyn

Mervyn Noel (twins) Maxine Kay
~Barbara   ~Thomas MARKOW

Lianne Yvonne
~Graham John COWLAND

Joanne
~? McFARLANE

Kay
~?McCULLOUGH

Sheree Renae

Duran Corey

Kylie Nicole

Angela

Anne Shirley
~Robert WAREHAM

Dennis Edwin
~Kerry Underwood

Judy Mary

Sandra Helen
~Frank BORG

Derrylee Roma
~Terry BOTTRELL

Jamie Belinda Anne   Kilely   Jenny Shiree

Roger Wayne

Scott Dean

Amelia

Ashley   Adelle

Patricia Ann
~Ian HILL

Lyell Brenton
~Melanie Dekoning

Beverly Jan

Karen Fay

Map indicating Place-names in South Australia

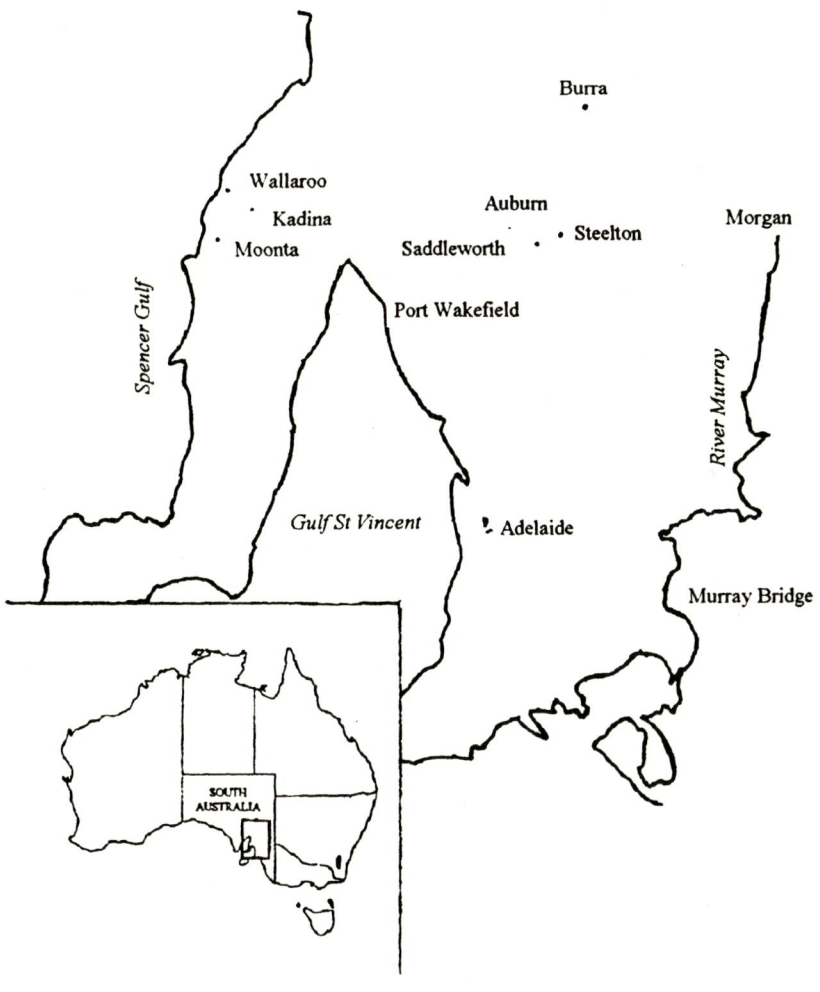

Map indicating Place-names in England

Index

Printed in the United Kingdom
by Lightning Source UK Ltd.
105046UKS00001B/259-297